Penguin
LIVES

SAINT AUGUSTINE

A LIPPER/VIKING BOOK

GARRY WILLS

SAINT AUGUSTINE

A Penguin Life

A LIPPER/VIKING BOOK

VIKING

Published by the Penguin Group
Penguin Putnam Inc., 375 Hudson Street,
New York, New York 10014, U.S.A.
Penguin Books Ltd, 27 Wrights Lane, London W8 5TZ, England
Penguin Books Australia Ltd, Ringwood, Victoria, Australia
Penguin Books Canada Ltd, 10 Alcorn Avenue,
Toronto, Ontario, Canada M4V 3B2
Penguin Books (N.Z.) Ltd, 182–190 Wairau Road,
Auckland 10, New Zealand
Penguin India, 210 Chiranjiv Tower,
43 Nehru Tower, New Delhi 11009, India

Penguin Books Ltd, Registered Offices:
Harmondsworth, Middlesex, England

First published in 1999 by Viking Penguin,
a member of Penguin Putnam Inc.

7   9   10   8

LIBRARY OF CONGRESS CATALOGING-IN-PUBLICATION DATA
Wills, Garry.
Saint Augustine / Garry Wills.
p.   cm.
"A Penguin life."
ISBN 0-670-88610-6
1. Augustine, Saint. Bishop of Hippo.   2. Christian saints—Algeria—
Hippo (Extinct city)—Biography.   I. Title.
BR1720.A9W55   1999
270.2'092—dc21   98–50317

This book is printed on acid-free paper.

(∞)

Printed in the United States of America
Set in Minion
Designed by Francesca Belanger

TO FANNIA

gone but with us

ACKNOWLEDGMENTS

My deepest debt is to James O'Donnell, not only for his great three-volume edition of the *Confessiones,* or his Augustine Web site, but for the generosity with which he read and improved my manuscript. My thanks go again to my conscientious typist, Joan Stahl. Also to my agent, Andrew Wylie.

INTRODUCTION

Augustine thinks in questions.
—KARL JASPERS

A WORD FROM HIS INMOST BEING goes direct to our most guarded self: "My heart's fellow will love in me what You [Lord] tell us is lovable, deplore in me what You tell us is deplorable" (T 10.5). Yet this man with such modern access to us was considered peripheral in his day, a provincial on the margins of classical culture. He did not even speak Greek, the language of the international intelligentsia. His contemporary critic Julian of Eclanum called him a guru of the outback, "what passes for a philosopher with Africans" (U 5.11). Stranded in ancient Numidia (modern Algeria), the country of his birth, Augustine was for thirty-five years the bishop of a modest port city, Hippo Regius, where he could only be (in Julian's sophisticated sneer) "the donkey protector" to fellow Africans (U 4.56). We should not make too much of Augustine's church office—there were almost seven hundred bishops in Africa alone, where one was consecrated on the average every week (VDM 11, 225). Augustine went into the later iconography of his church wearing all the episcopal finery of the late Middle Ages—miter, crozier, gloves, ring, and so on. But he dressed in the gray clothes of a monk, and celebrated the rites of his church in that everyday garb.

His influence came not from his ecclestical rank, but from his writings, which were staggering in quantity—his own incomplete review of his books numbered ninety-three. There are, besides, almost three hundred of his letters and over four hundred sermons (out of the estimated eight thousand that he preached). What he said of the learned pagan Varro was even truer of him: "Though he read so much that we are amazed he found time to write, he wrote so much that few, we believe, can have read it all" (CG 6.2). Augustine dictated to relays of stenographers, often late into the night (L 139.3, 224.2). He employed teams of copyists. His sermons, several a week, were taken down by his own or others' shorthand writers. In some seasons, he preached daily. His letters were sent off in many copies. He paced about as he dictated, a reflection of the mental restlessness and energy conveyed in the very rhythms of his prose (VDM 414).

He was a tireless seeker, never satisfied. Like Aeneas, the hero of his favorite poem, he sailed toward ever-receding shores (*Aeneid* 6.61). Impatient with all preceding formulations, even his own, he was drawn to and baffled by mystery: "Since it is God we are speaking of, you do not understand it. If you could understand it, it would not be God." (S 117.5) We seek one mystery, God, with another mystery, ourselves. We are mysterious to ourselves *because* God's mystery is in us: "Our mind cannot be understood, even by itself, because it is made in God's image" (S 398.2).

Augustine's description of the human urgency toward truth was an unwitting exercise in self-portraiture:

> The impulse present in our seeking goes out beyond the seeker, and hovers as it were, unable to rest in any other goal until what is sought has been found and the seeker is united with it. This impulse, or search, does not seem to be love, which we have for known things, since it is an effort toward the unknown. Yet it has a quality cognate to love's. It can be called an act of will, for the seeker wills to find, and if something knowable is being sought, then the seeker has a will to know. If that seeking is urgent and focused, it is called studious—our term for those wanting to master knowledge. So an impulse of some kind precedes the mind's generative act, and through this will to seek and find knowledge, the knowledge itself comes to birth. (Trin 9.18)

This restlessness outward is what Augustine called "the unstable heart" (*cor inquietum*), tumbling humans off balance toward what they want, without knowing what it is. "Our yearning anticipates landfall, throws hope as an anchor toward that shore" (P 64.3).

His mind was always refashioning what it found inadequate. This dynamic character to his thought has been missed by those who break it off at any point and treat it as a system. The medieval period misunderstood *The City of God* as a fixed doctrine of church-state relations. Calvin tied down with an iron logic what is a dialectical *process* in Augustine's thought on grace. The attitude of Augustine was one of joint endeavor after a truth that is always just beyond us:

Let the reader, where we are equally confident, stride on with me; where we are equally puzzled, pause to investigate with me; where he finds himself in error, come to my side; where he finds me erring, call me to his side. So we may keep to the path, in love, as we fare on toward Him "whose face is ever to be sought." (Trin 1.5)

If others could advance beyond his capacities, he urged them to do so:

Press on where you can. When we reach our final destination, you will not have to question me, nor I you. We are presently seeking in faith what we shall then share joyfully in vision. (S 261.3)

Calvin had an exalted misconception of Augustine—an understandable misunderstanding, as it were. A more superficial but very common view of Augustine turns the great seeker into nothing but the great sinner, an ex-debauchee obsessed with sex. The title of his best-known book contributes to this reductive treatment of the man. *Confessiones,* transliterated rather than translated into English *Confessions,* misses the complexity of a word in which Augustine intuited an entire theology. It is the accepted view that *confessio* had three main meanings in Augustine: confession of sin, praise of God, and profession of faith (A-L "Confessio" col. 1122). But the word has a wider range, with less rigid boundaries, than this schema can suggest. *Confiteri* means, etymologically, to *cor*roborate, to *con*firm testimony, and even inanimate things can do that—Augustine's fellow African Apuleius said that "jewels confess [confirm the status of] the grande dame." Augustine himself says that the inanimate universe confesses (testifies to) God (T 10.9). The thing confessed does not have to be a moral truth—Augustine "confesses" the fact that time is measurable (T 11.33). The term that best covers this range of meanings for *confessio* is "testimony" (*testimonium* is used twice in the second sentence of the *Confessiones*).

All this is distant from the atmosphere of "confessions" in modern English—which is suggestive either of criminal surrender (as in *True Confessions* literature) or of the medieval penitentiary system ("going to confession"). But criminal confession in Augustine's time was usually coerced by torture, and the penitential system of the church "confessional" did not exist then. In the fourth century, once sin was washed away by baptism, the Christian was expected to live free of grave sins. One lapse could lead to a one-time public penitence and a formal reacceptance into the Church. But a second lapse meant permanent exclusion from the Church.

Augustine was not confessing like an Al Capone, or like a pious trafficker of later confessionals. In fact, his use of the term is so broad, one can ask why he bothers to insist that he *is* testifying, since everything, whether it knows it or not, testifies to God. Even demons "confess" (acknowledge) God by their opposition to Him. So do heretics. Inanimate things proclaim their creator: "Their beauty is their testimony"—*Pulchritudo eorum confessio eorum* (S 241.2). Obviously man's whole life testifies in this way (P 30.11).

Then why does Augustine use this general term for what he is doing in a particular book? The answer, as so often with Augustine, lies in Scripture. His favorite part of the Jewish Scriptures, the Psalms, says that man articulates the universal testimony to God. "Confess" and "testify" are used interchangeably for the witness that His believers must give the Lord:

> The tribes of Israel go up to Jerusalem, and because "there is no falsehood in them," those tribes are in themselves the "testimony [*testimonium*] of Israel." Whither do they go up, and why? "To testify [*confiteri*] to your name, Lord." It could not be more eloquently put. Pride asserts, humility testifies [*confitetur*]. The proud want to seem what they are not. The one who gives testimony [*confessor*] does not want to appear what he is not, but to love what, in the full sense, is. (P 121.8)

And Augustine's favorite Gospel in the Christian Scriptures, John's, says that the Son must testify to the Father, as the Spirit does to the Son. Christians are brought into the inmost mystery of the Trinity when the Spirit testifies in them to the triune glory: "As the Spirit gave them an inner testimony of Christ, they spread the testimony themselves" (S 94.2). It is this action of the Spirit in Christians that Augustine wants to manifest: "This it is to testify [*confiteri*], to speak out what the heart holds true. If the tongue and the heart are at odds, you are reciting, not testifying" (J 26.2).

Little if any of this rich theological resonance carries over to the word "confessions" in English. That is why, unsettling as it is to many, I translate *Confessiones* as *The Testimony* of Augustine (with T as the key to citations of it). Better a shock of the new than indulging old associations that mislead.

We must be on guard from the outset for such misreadings, since Augustine seems deceptively easy of access. People feel, for instance, that they understand intuitively Augustine's testimony to his own sexual sins. In fact, they are convinced that Augustine was a libertine before his conversion, and was so obsessed with sex after his conversion that they place many unnamed sins to his account—though his actual sexual activity was not shocking by any standards but those of a saint. He lived with one woman for fifteen years "and with her alone, since I kept faith with her bed" (T 4.2). This kind of legal concubine was recognized in Roman law—a man who took another's concubine could be prosecuted as an adulterer. Even the Church recognized the legitimacy of such a relationship (Council of Toledo 400, Canon 17).

Yet the expectation of sexual excess in Augustine's life leads people to add sexual scenes and themes to his story—incestuous feelings for his mother or homosexual feelings for his friend. The obsessive treatment of Augustine's supposed sexual obsession is apparent in two well-known and repeatedly cited articles by modern psychiatrists. They discuss the scene where Augustine's father sees him nude in the public baths and rejoices that he will become a grandfather, since Augustine had reached sexual maturity. "My childhood past," Augustine says, "[I was] clothed in unstable manhood [*inquieta adulescentia*]" (T 2.6). Dr. Charles Klingerman takes that adjective *inquieta* to mean Augustine had an erection in the baths. Drs. R. Brändle and W. Neidhart go further, supposing that Augustine's father saw him masturbating.

Such academic conjecture is based on many kinds of ignorance. The authors are unaware of facts like these:

1. The Roman baths were public gathering places, more like our present shopping malls than later "Turkish baths," and a strict decorum was expected there (O'Donnell 2.120). Even the nuns entrusted to Bishop Augustine's care had their regular day at the baths (VDM 224).

2. St. Augustine thought, apparently from experience, that public exposure of the genitals is a *detumescing* experience (CG 14.20), not one to cause erection.

3. This third period of Augustine's life (*adulescentia*) is clearly marked according to a system dear to him, whereby the six ages of man corresponded with the six stages of history and the six days of creation. It stretches from age sixteen to thirty. It is *not* "adolescence" as we use that term (O'Donnell 2.52–56).

4. The adjective *inquieta* is Augustine's regular word for the instability of the heart that draws one to God in a system of spiritual "throw weights" (*pondera*).

5. This adjective is applied to the period of Augustine's life, not to his penis. Drs. Brändle and Neidhart solve the problem by changing the adjective into a noun (Augustine's impulse, *Drang*, affecting his body, *Leib*). They entirely neglect the adjective *indutum* (wearing), though this is clearly the oddest word in the sentence: he is nude in the baths, yet he says that he is *clothed*.

6. Augustine connected the word *indutum* with baptism, where the nude initiate was totally immersed in Augustine's time and came out of the water "wearing Christ" (S 216.2). The "old man" was put off to be *clothed* in Christ's identity.

7. This term is taken from the very text of Saint Paul that tipped the balance at the scene of Augustine's own conversion

(T 8.29): "Be clothed (*induite*) in Christ Jesus" (Romans 13.14), leading to his baptism by Saint Ambrose.

8. Adam, naked in Eden, had no shame in his body as it came from God. Before the fall, his nakedness wore the clothing (*indutamentum*) of grace (CG 14.17). That innocence is regained when the grace of Christ is put on.

9. The informal inspection by Augustine's father is a parallel to the formal "physical" (*scrutatio*) given candidates for baptism to ensure bodily integrity (S 216.10–11). The candidate for baptism went through Lent in a penitential garb, unable to bathe until Thursday of Holy Week, when he or she went to the public baths to prepare for the *scrutatio* in church.

So the odd word "clothed," in this scene of nakedness, is the key to the whole passage. Augustine in the public baths is a fallen Adam, not yet clothed in Christ's grace—as he will be when Ambrose immerses him in the *spiritual* bath of baptism. The two pool scenes form a kind of diptych, one concerned with care of the body under a worldly father's gaze, the other cleansing the soul with a recognition of God's paternity.

What happens to that scene in the pages of the psychiatrists occurs all too often when people do not take Augustine's theology seriously. The bishop is concerned with the mysteries of grace, water, and salvation, with the "old Adam" and the new, with a deeper "scrutiny" and final paternity—while his modern readers are indulging their own fantasies about a hyperactive penis. This poses a barrier to knowing the real Augustine.

But some will find a difficulty in Augustine's highly symbolic way of telling his story. Are his memories so buried in layer upon layer of scriptural language or theological reflection that the original event loses its specificity, perhaps even its trustworthiness? The fear of this led some people to resent Pierre Courcelle's pathfinding work on Augustine's use of biblical symbols. But the fear is unfounded, for two reasons.

First, Augustine sincerely experienced his memories as drenched in God's grace, which makes the memories testify, belatedly, to God. This was, in his view, the most truthful report on his experience. To ask him for something else is to demand that he *not* be authentic in his life as he had come to understand it.

Second, once we accept and understand his theological language, previously unsuspected information about his life, even at the literal biographical level, can be retrieved from *The Testimony*. I shall be arguing, for instance, that he tells us far more about his mistress, and about the son they conceived and raised, than earlier biographers have recognized. When he talks about his sins, he is often speaking in very specific ways about those two people. He was not particularly interested in giving us literal details of his biography. But he could not keep from doing so indirectly. That is the story I shall be ferreting out in the first half of this book, the part that is covered by *The Testimony*.

SAINT AUGUSTINE

I

AFRICA (354–383)

1. Thagaste: 354–366

MOUNTAINS HE HAD KNOWN from boyhood, but not the sea. Thagaste, his birthplace in North Africa (modern Souk Ahras), was sixty miles inland from the Mediterranean, sealed off by the nearby Medjerda mountain range. To the south, the more distant Aures chain separated him from the Saharan desert. Mountains would always be part of his mental landscape—symbols of God's stability or of skyward reach in John's Gospel. But toward the sea he had to grope with mental inference. Asked in later life, by a friend from his hometown, how one can "remember" things never experienced, he admitted that no one can recall a strawberry's flavor who has not tasted one. But the concept of water with a boundary is as close as the nearest drinking cup (L 7). So Virgil's hero Aeneas would be struggling with tempests in a water cup when Augustine first read the *Aeneid*. He was born into a world very contained.

Numidia was part of the Roman Empire, whose signs were all around Augustine as he was growing up—the straight stone-rooted roads, the striding aqueducts, the peopled amphitheaters.

1

Along its northern rim, the empire was troubled by "barbarians" and by theological wars (the high theology and low skullduggery of fights over Arianism). But this southern edge of the empire was secure. Known as Rome's granary, Numidia was separated from desert nomads by a long ditch (the Fossa) that defined Rome's jurisdiction as clearly as did Hadrian's Wall in the empire's far north. Augustine would have assumed, like his parents, that the Roman order was eternal. Even as he was dying at age seventy-six, he had trouble accepting the collapse of a political order he considered providential. Remember, Rome had been *Christian* since 313, and *Christian* Visigoths were besieging Hippo.

Thagaste was securely Catholic by 354, when Augustine was born there. But it had been controlled, during his mother's girlhood, by Donatists, those Christian puritans (named for their leaders, Donatus) who revered the martyrs of Diocletian's persecution and would not be reconciled with any who had compromised in the time of trial (L 93.17). W. H. C. Frend, the historian of Donatism, thinks that Augustine's Catholic mother was raised in the atmosphere of that sect. Her name, like that of many Donatists, is Berber—its proper form is Monnica, related to the old Libyan god Mon, who was worshiped in nearby Thibilis. Her devotion to martyr shrines was the specialty, in Africa, of the Donatists. Augustine followed Berber custom when he called his son Godsend (Adeodatus in Latin), though Augustine never learned the Berber language spoken by his country's manual laborers. His parents and the slaves who brought him up spoke only Latin to him, since he was destined for the Roman bureaucracy in which his father held minor local office.

That father, Patrick (Patricius), had "curial" rank—he was a decurion, a town councilor with tax-collecting duties, and not a Christian. Augustine calls him meager in his land holdings (*tenuis,* T 2.5), but that was the typical stance of his class. As the historian of the empire A. H. M. Jones writes: "We never hear of a contented decurion." They were bound down to their land and their duties, and so were their heirs—Augustine escaped only by selling his inheritance when he became a bishop (L 126.7). Patrick's vineyards were worked by slaves, and Augustine had a slave attendant (pedagogue) who took him to school (T 1.30).

Augustine tells us practically nothing about himself before the age of eleven or twelve when he went to live with his pedagogue in a neighboring town with a secondary school. But we can find traces in his later writing of the bright-eyed and observant boy he must have been. The principal art form of Roman Africa was mosaic work—he mentions the rich mosaics owned by his own patron in Thagaste, Romanian. He would later think of order in the universe on the model of his hometown's mosaics:

> If a person were to look at an intricate pavement so narrowly as to see only the single *tesserae,* he would say the artist, lacking a sense of composition, had set the little pieces at haphazard, since he could not take in at once the whole pattern, inlaid to form a single image of beauty (O 1.2).

Even in his seventies, Augustine would still be thinking of divine order in terms of mosaics: "Order disposes all things, regular and irregular, in the places they fit" (CG 19.13).

Augustine hated school and played truant to see games—the

bear-baiting shows put on by Romanian, or the fighting cocks to be seen in a splendid mosaic found near Carthage. Though Augustine was later very critical of games in the arena, some bloodsports of his youth kept their hold on him. Even while he was preparing for baptism he could write:

> We saw gamecocks sharpening toward a scrap. We *had* to watch, for what horizon do eyes of love not scan, hoping for a hint of reason's beautiful scheme, which checks and impels all things (whether they realize it or not), a scheme that makes its observer quick to respond whenever it beckons? It can flash its signals out of anything, in anything. In, for instance, these cocks: the thrust of their heads toward battle, their lifted crests, their darting attacks, skilled parries; pure animal action without mind, yet how apt, every move; for a higher mind works through them, ordering all things. At the last, the victor's right: the exultant crowing, a body taut with pride of power. And the rites of defeat—limp wings, carriage and croak gone awry; all strangely fitting and, by their consonance with nature's set way, beautiful. (O 1.25)

And a dozen years later he wrote: "I no longer go to the arena to see a hound chase a hare. But if by chance I catch sight of that in a field, the hunt attracts me, distracts my concentration from the most important matters. It reins aside not my horse but my heart's regard." (T 10.57)

Thagaste, though not near the sea or a navigable river, was crisscrossed by major land routes, which meant that Augustine saw in its streets Berber faces from the desert as well as the

Semitic features of Africa's ancient Phoenician settlers (Perler 120–21). He would later marvel at God's ability to differentiate people using the same limited features of eyes, nose, and mouth. Like other Mediterraneans, the citizens of Thagaste shunned the midday heat and lingered out conviviality through the night. When he became sixteen, Augustine relates, he and his friends roamed the streets looking for trouble after dusk, and saved their worst pranks till after midnight (T 2.9). But that was after he had returned from Madauros.

2. Madauros: 366–370

SINCE AUGUSTINE does not mention the town where he attended secondary school until book 2 of *The Testimony*, many readers have associated the account of his school days in book 1 with Thagaste. But he talks, in book 1, of studying Virgil and failing in his Greek lessons—the curriculum of grammar school, which Augustine must have entered when he was eleven or twelve for him to complete the course when he was sixteen, the age he gives for his return from Madauros (Perler 126).

Though Madauros (near present Mdaourouch) was only sixteen miles from Thagaste as the crow flies, the road there was roundabout and difficult, like most land travel in Numidia. One had to descend into the Medjerda Valley and go up onto the central plains, the great wheat and barley fields that made up Rome's granary (Perler 126–27). Madauros took pride in being a sophisticated town in a backward area. The poorer classes of the region, largely Donatist, kept up the cult of martyrs with uncouth names mocked by the educated—names like Miggin, Sanamen, Namphano (L 16). But statues of pagan gods were honored in the forum. Christian Africans might look back to their great orator of the third century, Saint Cyprian. But Madauros boasted of its fellow townsman of the second century, Apuleius, the naughty novelist of *The Golden Ass*.

Archaeological finds show that there was a flourishing paganism in Madauros—the town had profited from the reign of the neopagan emperor Julian, whose life ended just three years before Augustine went there (Lepelley 1.98–101, 2.128–29). With the exception of Julian's brief reign (361–363), the empire had been formally Christian since Constantine's decree of toleration in 313. But pagan offices and titles survived—Augustine's friend and patron in Thagaste, Romanian, held the pagan title of priest *(flamen)*. Education for all those who aspired to influence was still in the pagan classics, a situation later deplored by Augustine but accepted without question by his parents. The result was a curious mixture of religious sensibilities. As historian Arnoldo Momigliano put it: "Adam and Eve and what followed [in the Bible] had in some way to be presented in a world populated by Deucalion, Cadmus, Romulus, and Alexander the Great." For many, this religio-mythical mixture never did get sorted out. When Augustine was bishop he had to rebuke members of his congregation who could say: "Just because I frequent idols and get advice from visionaries and fortune tellers, that does not mean I have left the church—I am a Catholic!" (P 88.2.14).

It is against such confusion that we must read Augustine's harsh criticism of his teachers and his parents for bringing him into the pagan system of myths and poetry during his boyhood. He received them eagerly: "My ears were inflamed for pagan myths, and the more they were scratched the more they itched" (T 1.16). He was assigned such inflammatory tales, not only to read but to enact—he had to impersonate Juno in a public declamation of his own composition. Though he was told the situation was fictitious, he was supposed to make the goddess's passions as realistic as possible.

It was all too real for him. He loved Virgil, and wrote of him in *The City of God* (1.3):

> It is hard to aerate minds brimmed with him in impressionable years, as Horace says:
>> *A cask's first wine, into it fit,*
>> *Long afterwards will breathe of it.*

He suffered with Dido, his fellow African, when she was deserted by Aeneas—as Augustine was abandoned by the parents who sent him off to Madauros. He could direct Dido's call for vengeance (*Aeneid* 4.625) to the teachers who beat him for not learning Greek: "Rise from my ashes some avenging Wrath." The adolescent Augustine entered so ardently into the mythical system of Virgil that he convinced at least one sophisticated pagan in Madauros that he, too, was a pagan. This older man, an intimate of Augustine's during his sojourn in Madauros, wrote to Augustine after the latter's conversion, noting that he now paid homage to mumbo-jumbo Christian martyrs like Miggin and Namphano.

We have only one letter from this correspondent, Maximus, with Augustine's answer to it, but references in the letters indicate that there was correspondence preceding them, and (probably) following. The tone is one of joshing familiarity on both sides. Maximus asks Augustine not to dazzle him with his customary rhetoric, but to argue seriously:

> Eager as ever for the joy of hearing from you—for the energy of your words that recently gave me, in all charity, a pleasant pommeling—I am not loath to answer in kind (L 16).

Augustine pretends that Maximus must be joking if he thinks that lascivious pagan gods are more admirable than men who died for their faith:

> Are we engaged in something serious here, or is it time to tell jokes? I cannot judge, from the tone of your letter, whether you prefer wit to pertinency because your arguments are weak or because you are, as usual, so affable. (L 17)

Hasn't Maximus noticed where he lives?

> How can you forget who you are, an African addressing Africans (we are both in Africa, you know), that you find Phoenician names so despicable?

Since Augustine lumped the Berber and Phoenician languages together, he thought his mother's name was Phoenician—like

Dido's. His own love of his country comes out in this rebuke to Maximus:

> If the Phoenician language offends you, and you deny (what the most learned admit) that much wisdom survives in Phoenician documents, then you must be ashamed of your birthplace, the cradle of that language.

Augustine calls Maximus his elder. Was he a teacher or just an originally revered mentor? He was, at any rate, in a position to say that Augustine was of his religious party (*secta*). We can gauge from that the depth of Augustine's seduction by pagan literature, and understand better his later denunciation of those who exposed him to it. He knew what power the pagan poets had—they had, for a while, made him a pagan.

Attended only by his pedagogue in Madauros, Augustine was able to get his way, telling lies to pedagogue, teacher, and parents to avoid school and slip off to games in the amphitheater (T 1.30). When he *was* forced to attend school, he hated the flogging system upheld by parents and universal custom. Despite the lash, he refused to learn Greek—not because he could not, but because he *would* not learn it this way.

He had learned Latin quickly because his "heart was laboring to express itself," but with Greek his "unfettered inquisitiveness" was checked by "intimidating assignments" (T 1.23). Later he dutifully repented his stubbornness, but his schoolfellows probably admired his proud resistance despite repeated floggings. The lack of Greek severely limited him in later days—though even this he managed to turn into a partial advantage. His deep originality comes in part from his lack of dependence on other traditions.

3. Thagaste: 370–371

WHEN AUGUSTINE RETURNED from school in Madauros, he entered the stage of life, earlier mentioned (from age sixteen to thirty), that Romans called *adulescentia.* He was supposed to go on to higher education in rhetoric, but his father did not, at the moment, have enough money to support such studies in Carthage. So Augustine spent his crucial sixteenth year in his hometown, where he initiated the sexual activity his father saw he was capable of and his mother warned him against. His mother was practical about it, hoping he would keep entirely chaste, but telling him at the least not to have affairs with married women (T 2.6).

It has always amazed people that, in this year of burgeoning sexual desire, the sin he concentrated on—spending over half of book 2 of *The Testimony* on an introspective analysis of it—is the theft of some pears. Why spill so many words on what many dismiss as a child's petty theft?

It was more than that to Augustine. In fact, he had dismissed with passing mention earlier thefts of food from his family larder, food used to to bribe others into letting him play with them (T 1.30). That theft had a motive. The pear theft seemed not to. He specifically says he had legitimate access to more and better pears (probably on Romanian's estate). He did not want to eat or use the stolen goods. He and his fellows in the raid carted the fruit off and dumped it before pigs. Why did they do it? Augustine goes down and down into the mystery of this apparent *acte gratuit:* "Simply what was not allowed allured us" (*eo liberet quo non liceret,* T 2.9).

He tries out and rejects an explanation from his school readings, one fresh in mind at that time. Sallust, one of the four canonical authors in the grammar studies he had just completed, was a favorite author in Africa, because he wrote the history of an African conflict (*The Jugurthine War*). In another book, *The Conspiracy of Catiline,* Sallust said that Catiline led a gang of young men in senseless criminal exercises because he was "gratuitously evil" (16).

But Augustine remembers that Sallust, in the very same place, contradicts himself, admitting that the "pointless" crimes *did* have a point. They were indulged in "lest hand or heart lose edge for lack of practice." Little meannesses were like the finger exercises of a pianist. Catiline was using them to prepare for the great criminal concerto of his attempt to take over the republic.

Was there anything similar in the act of Augustine's fellows? If not, Augustine would have to think that humans can choose evil for its own sake. In writing *The Testimony,* he recognizes that people always do bad things in pursuit of apparent good. But what possible good was there in the pear theft, an act as silly as it was mean-spirited? He lists all the reasons for committing other sins. Those who have suspected a sexual symbolism behind Augustine's horror at his vandalism ignore Augustine's own statement that the act would not have been mysterious if sex were discoverable in it:

> The beauty of physical things is appealing (gold, silver and the rest), and we sway in response to what touches the flesh or affects any of the senses by its fitness to them. There is a dignity in worldly respect, in the power to order others about or to persuade them (whence comes the appetite for subduing them). Yet to gain even these good things we should not give up you, God, nor wander from your law. Our life in this world is tempting because it accommodates us to its order, patterned to beautiful (if lower) things. Friendship, for instance, forms a sweet bond because it creates a harmony of the several souls. Sin arises from this, and from things like this, only if a disordered fastening on lowest goods makes us fall from higher goods, from the highest of all, you my God, my lord, your truth, your law. . . . When the motive for a crime is sought, none is accepted but the desire to get goods of the lower sort just mentioned, or to avoid their loss. For they *are* beautiful, they *do* please, even if they must be abandoned for, or subordinated to, higher and more fulfilling goods. A murder is committed. Why? To get another's wife or wealth, or to get the necessities of life. Or for fear another would deprive the murderer of such things. Or from a sense of wrong burning for redress. Who murders with no cause but to enjoy the mere murdering? Who would credit such a motive? (T 2.10)

In his exhaustive search for some conceivable good to be found in his bad act, Augustine finally comes up with a psychological clue: Whatever his motive for acting with the gang, he would not have done the same thing all by himself. Does that suggest some good hidden in the bad? He finds a psychological parallel that may help him toward an explanation. People normally laugh when together, not when alone—or, as Bergson put it, anyone who laughs alone is *imagining* the company of others (*Le Rire* 1). There is something essentially social about laughter. Companionship (*consortium*) is the good in the morally indifferent act of laughing. Could that have been the good paradoxically prompting him to the bad act of theft? Yes, he concludes: "The mutual provocation of my partners in crime provided the friction that ignited my desire to act thus" (T 2.16).

He began his discussion with the observation that theft is *obviously* wrong, since even thieves do not want to be stolen from. He will later dwell on the bonds of good that unite even robber bands; they insist on just distribution of the "take" from their robberies (CG 19.12). *Consortium* and *amicitia* (friendship) are key values in Augustine's eyes. His later companionship with heretics will prolong his own adherence to error. He will make *amicitia* the base of all Christian communities. He will even dispute Cicero's definition of the state, saying that "things *loved* in common" are the basis of all politics, not mere abstract justice. So a persistent love of fellowship was the falsely conceived good behind his motiveless act in the pear orchard. Augustine has solved his own psychological mystery without having to resort to the Manichean heresy, which holds that evil is a positive (choosable) substance.

But more. People notice that there is a parallel between this "first sin" of *The Testimony* and Adam's fall in the garden of Eden. Though the gang hauls off a "huge load" (*onera ingentia*) of pears from the orchard, Augustine talks of only one tree—like the tree of the apple in Eden. He goes out of his way to say the pears were not beautiful, marking a contrast with the fruit in Eden, where the tree "was pleasant to the eyes" (Genesis 3.6). But a further parallel, the key one, has not been noticed, I think. Eve falls for the serpent's lies in Genesis; but Saint Paul's First Letter to Timothy (which Augustine thought was authentically Pauline) says that "Adam was not deceived" (2.14). Why did Adam commit the original sin if he was neither desirous of the fruit in itself nor deceived about any power it might give him? The problem is exactly Augustine's in his own little orchard.

Augustine argued, in his treatment of the Genesis story, that Adam committed his sin deliberately in order to maintain his "bond of company" (*socialis necessitudo,* CG 14.11) with Eve. In the book *First Meanings in Genesis,* which he began while finishing *The Testimony,* he wrote of Adam's misguided gallantry (11.59):

> After Eve had eaten from the forbidden tree and offered him its fruit to eat along with her, Adam did not want to disappoint her, when he thought she might be blighted without his comforting support, banished from his heart to die sundered from him. He was not overcome by disordered desire of the flesh, which he had not yet experienced as a thing in his body at odds with his mind, but by a kind of amicable desire for another's good [*amicali quadam benivolentia*], which often happens,

making us sin against God so as not to turn a friend [*amicus*] against us.

Augustine's point is that Adam helps neither Eve nor himself by trying to separate off a lower love from the Source of love. *That* is the lesson he finds in his own courting of favor from his fellow thieves in the pear orchard. He sees here his own distant echo of Adam's sin, the primordial sin, the quest for love by motion *away* from the one place where it can be found.

To find the Genesis narrative coming alive in his own past is a continuing surprise for Augustine in *The Testimony.* We have seen that already in the story of his father and the public baths, when he was "clothed" in Adam's shame. We shall see it in other key episodes of the book, including the death of his friend and his prayer with Monnica at Ostia. Genesis haunts the whole work.

Augustine began, in book 2 (6), the account of his sexual activity at sixteen, only to break it off in his concentration on the pear episode. He resumes the sexual story at the beginning of book 3, which O'Donnell (2.145) rightly calls "recapitulative," though it is marked by his arrival in Carthage. It is in book 3 that he first mentions his concubine. But O'Donnell (2.207) draws an interesting conclusion from the age of Augustine's son:

Adeodatus was [almost fifteen] at the time of his baptism in the spring of 387 . . . and [aged sixteen] at the dramatic date of *The Teacher* not long after; on this calculation he was born 371/72, when Augustine was perhaps seventeen . . . or perhaps even 370, thus apparently probably in the first years of study at

Carthage *but conceivably during the years of indolence recorded at 2, 3.5–6* (the philoprogenitive optimism of Patricius did not have so long to wait). Adeodatus' mother was dismissed from Milan and returned to Africa in 385/6 . . . and thus shared his entire *adulescentia.*

I italicize the phrase about Augustine's year in Thagaste. If his son was conceived when Augustine was sixteen or seventeen, he would either have found that son's mother in his hometown or made a very quick discovery of her in Carthage. Theirs was not a casual attachment. He tells us how it tore him apart to lose her, and that he was faithful their whole fifteen years together: "I lived with only one women [*unam habebam*] and kept faith with her bed" (T 4.2). To avoid clumsy titles, where she has no name, I shall call this woman Una (from *unam habebat*). It is later revealed that Una was a Catholic, and Thagaste was a more Catholic town than Carthage. Besides, a very mysterious passage in book 3 (5) makes far better sense if we connect it with Una *and Thagaste.* Augustine writes that he committed one particularly monstrous sin in church, during the ceremonies, "desiring and effecting a transaction [*negotium*] whose fruit should have brought death" (T 3.5). That is all he says of the event, and people have supplied lurid guesses about what happened, some even having him accomplish intercourse during the service. Even soberer guesses are strange. Peter Brown (41) suggests that Augustine, a stranger in Carthage, was cruising a church "to find a girl friend." O'Donnell (2.159) finds it significant that Augustine was still going to church in Carthage.

But one did not just "drop in" to a fourth-century African church in a strange town. Membership was guarded jealously (among other things, to keep out the schismatic Donatists from the church down the street). Aspiring catechumens were confined to their special part of the liturgy, and baptized members had to maintain public morality or be expelled. It is far more likely that Augustine is talking about an event in the church of Thagaste, where his mother was a recognized member and he was a catechumen, and that the event, whatever it was, concerned Una.

Could "picking up" a woman (asking her for a date) justify the harsh language Augustine uses? It is interesting that he calls his union with Una another kind of "transaction," a *pactum* (4.2). Did he persuade Una to come live with him while they were at church? Or to go away with him to Carthage? Or to return to him after she had tried to break off their affair? Did he try to persuade her to use an abortifacient? He later says that their child was unwanted, by him at least (4.2).

Any one of these possibilities is far more probable than other suggestions that have been made. His treatment of Una would justify the self-condemning language Augustine uses. He was not merely persuading Una to live with him, but to make a break with her church (and, no doubt, her Catholic parents). Augustine would later reproach himself bitterly for trying to persuade a dear friend to give up Catholicism. Though the Church admitted some forms of legal concubinage, Augustine said (4.2) theirs was not such a union, since they did not intend to have children. And the lack of further offspring after the first shows that Augustine—against her will, he implies—used contraceptive strategies.

Later, as a bishop, Augustine would pose a case that was very clearly what his own life with Una had been, her faithfulness contrasted with his faithlessness on the basis of the intent to bear children.

> If a man lives with one woman for some time, but only until he finds another worthier in terms of rank or advantages, he commits adultery in his heart, not against the one he wants to claim but against the one he lived with, even though they were not married. As for the woman who had knowingly and willingly lived with him outside the marriage contract—if she was true to his bed [*tori fidem*—exactly the way Augustine described his faithfulness to Una's bed] and does not seek another partner, I could bring no evident charge of adultery against her. . . . In fact, she is better than many married mothers if, in her sexual relations she did what she could to have children, but had to submit against her will to the prevention of conception. (*What Is Good in Marriage* 5.5)

O'Donnell suggests that this passage has the feel of a thing Una or her family may have been expected to hear.

In his dramatic sixteenth year at home, Augustine developed a relationship that would last even longer than the one with Una, though it was ended with an emotional rupture (O'Donnell 2.381–82). That was with his influential friend, the Thagaste multimillionaire Romanian (Lepelley 2.178–82). In *The Testimony*, Augustine credits his father with trying to raise money for his further education in Carthage. But in the earlier *Answer to Skeptics* (2.2), he makes it clear that Romanian took over his education from the outset:

> When I lacked money in young manhood, and was ready to travel for my education, you opened your estate [*domus*] to me, your resources [*sumptus*], and, what is more than either, your heart [*animus*]. And when I was deprived of my father, you compensated for that by your patronage, encouragement, and financial help.

There was no other time when Augustine could have developed this close relation with his patron but the interval between his schooling in Madauros and the later studies in Carthage. Augustine was given the run of Romanian's vast estate. It was there, and not at his own house, that he could meet Una in the initial stage of their affair. Since Romanian had intellectual aspirations, his library would have interested Augustine. Since Romanian's plans for Augustine involved his ultimately teaching in Thagaste, and especially tutoring Romanian's sons, Augustine may have done some elementary tutoring of the sons as young boys. When Augustine writes that he had at his command "more and better pears" than those he stole, he must be referring to Romanian's orchards. Augustine (T 2.9) speaks only of his father's vineyard, not an orchard. The connection with Romanian makes all the more absurd his night raid on a poor orchard. A brilliant prodigy favored by the town patron by day, he aspired to be a street tough by night. We shall see the same contradictory urges in Carthage, where he consorts with the town troublemakers (the

"Subversives," *Eversores*) while doing his graduate work with diligence. An observer of human contradiction, Augustine was always his own best subject of study.

4. Carthage: 371–374

AUGUSTINE'S FAMOUS OPENING to book 3 contains a pun on *Carthago* and *sartago*, the contents of a cooking pan (O'Donnell 2.146): "To Carthage I came, all that cartage [*sartago*] of illicit loves sizzling around me." This is taken to be Augustine's initiation into a career of debauchery, a very short career if he is to find Una and have her son by the time he is seventeen. But look again at the passage that is supposed to describe his sexual rampage. It applies better to the life of a confused graduate student with an unwanted baby and a sexual partner submitting reluctantly to this form of union. Augustine's paragraph (1) is closer to Jerome's description of married life—"The swelling womb, the *torturing jealousy*, the financial strain" (L 22.2, emphasis added)—than to the memory of a Don Juan:

> The stream of fellowship [*amicitia*] I polluted with the dregs of lust, clouding its clarity with dark longing—all the while taking myself for an urbane and sophisticated fellow, though I was vile and dishonest. I was reckless for love, wanting to be its captive. Yet you, merciful God, in all your kindness, dashed a bitterness through my joys. *Loved as I was, and chained as I was*

in enjoyment, glad to be *bound by its troublesome ties,* I was also beaten with *burning rods of jealousy and suspicion,* with fears and wraths and quarrelings. (T 3.1, emphasis added)

Since Augustine says he polluted *amicitia,* Rebecca West assumed that Augustine had a homosexual affair with an *amicus.* But there is no reason to think *amicitia* could not refer to heterosexual love. Augustine described the past of Adam with Eve as an *amicalis* benevolence. *Amicitia* comes from the verb for love (*amo*), and Augustine always referred back to Cicero's definition of it: "A union at the divine and human level effected by benevolence and love" (*Answer to Skeptics* 3.13).

Some might think that Augustine could not be referring to a stable affair, since he says he did not know real love, just "the love of loving" (T 3.1). But he thinks no love real that seals out God— not even his own passionate love for the friend described in book 4. Besides, "loving love" is not a dismissive term for adolescent infatuation. It is the very definition of God, and "whoever loves God must also love love" (Trin 8.12). It is that ideal of love that Augustine polluted in his long, sinful affair with Una.

To Augustine's ambition, as he was introduced to Romanian's contacts at the entrepôt of Carthage, there was soon added the burden of an undesired baby. The man given premature responsibilities yearned for reckless adventures, though he admits he held back, and was ashamed that he did so at the time. The gangs who raided classrooms, who mocked the very life Augustine was being inducted into, drew from him perverse admiration:

"Subversives" was the pejorative (even hellish) nickname they gave themselves as a gesture of impudence. I associated with them, but was ashamed not to match their shamelessness—since I kept clear of their raids, though I moved in their circle and had friends there. (T 3.6)

Though his son was initially unwanted, Augustine the close observer was bound to be fascinated by this infant forced on his attention, his Godsend (Adeodatus). The famous description of his own infancy, in book 1 of *The Testimony,* is based, as he tells us, on hearsay and observation—with an emphasis on the latter.

In time I began to smile, only in my sleep at first, and later when awake—so it was said of me, and I believed it, since we observe the same thing in other babies, though I do not remember it [in my own case]. . . . I have learned how babies act from the ones I had occasion to observe, who, without having known me [as an infant], taught me more than the nurses who did know me.

What infant did Augustine have more "occasion to observe" than his own son? It is clear that book 1's shrewd description of infant behavior came from the father who brooded over Godsend's cradle in 371. Here (T 1.8) are the cries that disturbed his Carthage nights while he was at home studying, not running wild with the Subversives:

How to suck, to sleep when soothed, to cry when my body vexed me—this I knew, and no more. . . . Gradually I became aware of my surroundings, and wished to express my demands to those who could comply with them; but I could not, since the demands were within me, and their fulfillers, outside me, had no faculty for entering into my mind. So I worked my limbs and voice energetically, trying to enact something like my demands, to the best of my little (and little availing) ability. Then, when I was frustrated—because I was not understood or was demanding something harmful—I went into high dudgeon that adults did not obey a child, that free people were not my slaves. So I inflicted on them my revenge of wailing.

That Augustine has Godsend in mind when describing his own infancy can be established by the repetition in *The Testimony* of themes explored earlier in his dialogue *The Teacher*, which he conducted with Godsend when the latter was sixteen. Both texts are concerned with the way one learns in general, with words and how they signify, with the role of natural signs in establishing conventional signs, with memory and the self-teaching that it makes possible. Here, for instance, is *The Teacher* (1.33):

By noticing the times when the word "head," often repeated, was used, I realized that it referred to a thing I was familiar with from having seen it before. Until I made that connection, "head" was merely a noise to me. It became a sign when I recognized the *thing* it signified. But I learned not from the sign but from the reality. The sign is learned from prior knowledge of its object, instead of the reverse.

And here is *The Testimony* (1.13):

All by myself, using the brain you gave me, my God, after failing to get whatever I wanted from whomever I wanted it, because my screams and inarticulate noises did not work, I used my memory to grasp what was outside me. Whenever people named something and showed with physical action the *thing* that matched that sound, I would take note and store in memory the fact that they used this sound when they wanted to indicate that thing. It was clear they wanted to do this from the physical action that is a "body language" for all humans—facial expressions, winks or other bodily indicators that, linked with vocal articulations, reveal the mind's desire to get, retain, repel or evade something. The words I heard, used in the same way [with relation to the signified] no matter how surrounding words varied, I made a collection of [in memory], and, shaping my mouth to these conventions, I made my own will plain to others.

Augustine proudly shows off his son's prowess in *The Teacher,* while assuring us that he did not teach the boy. Boys learn with God's own inborn instruments. But, as usual with Augustine, love sets the atmosphere in which God's gifts work. The hatred of his father's and his teachers' beatings made Augustine adopt a different strategy for dealing with his own son (and, later, his students in the classroom and his colleagues in the monastery):

I learned [to speak] as a baby, not inhibited by fear of punishment, surrounded as I was by coddling nurses, laughing games, and happy play. I learned without others' punitive insistence that I learn, from my own heart's need to deliver what I was laboring forth [*parienda*] to the outer world. . . . I picked up words from anyone who spoke to me, not just from tutors, and I somehow did labor forth my feelings in others' ears. Unfettered inquisitiveness, it is clear, teaches better than do intimidating assignments. (T 1.23)

Augustine's dialogue *Order in the Universe,* composed near the time of *The Teacher,* can be taken as one long illustration of that passage on Augustine's learning in an atmosphere of love. Dealing with young disciples in the dialogue on order, Augustine uses whatever piques the students' interest—odd noises in a drainpipe, gamecocks, enthusiastic singing in an outhouse—to circle back to the subject of order in the universe.

Yet permissive as Augustine was in his pedagogy, he was not starry-eyed about the human drives evidenced in the cradle. He notes the infant's demands for attention, the envy and anger at other infants competing for that attention. The urge to rule (*libido dominandi*) is the devil's first sin of pride and the cause of Adam's fall, whose traces show in every heir to that primal sin.

Despite all this, Godsend, the unwanted child, soon captivated his father and became a kind of laboratory experiment in the wonders of the human mind's development. This is the boy of whom Augustine wrote, "His talent, if a father's fondness deceives me not, was full of promise" (*Happiness in This Life* 1.6).

Book 3 of *The Testimony* tells us nothing of Augustine's intellectual development during his first two years in Carthage. But then, when he was nineteen, he came across Cicero's dialogue *Hortensius* (now lost) in the course of his rhetorical studies, and what follows is presented in a neat scheme: converted to "philosophy" by Cicero, Augustine goes to the Christian Scriptures for wisdom but is repelled by their crudity, so he explores the philosophy offered by Manicheism. This makes retrospective sense as Augustine arranges the three moral philosophies available to him at the time: pagan rationalism, Christian "superstition," Manichean mysticism. But he did not go seeking for Manichean doctrines from scratch. Later passages make it clear that he had come to know a very attractive group of young Manicheans from early in his stay at Carthage (perhaps when using the introductions of Romanian to influential people). These Manicheans, intellectual but fun-loving, exercised a counter-attraction, more humane and learned, to the rakish glamour of the Subversives. Here is Augustine's description of his graduate-school fellows:

> Their other qualities [other than their doctrine] more compelled my heart—conversation and laughter and mutual deferrings; shared readings of sweetly-phrased books, facetiousness alternating with things serious; heated arguing (as if with oneself), to spice our general agreement with dissent; teaching and being taught by turns; the sadness at anyone's absence, and the joy of return. Reciprocated love uses such semaphorings—a smile, a glance, a thousand winning acts—to fuse separate sparks into a single glow, no longer many souls, but one. (T 4.17)

This *jeunesse dorée* is described with all the intoxicated warmth of Evelyn Waugh's Oxford memories. No other aspect of Augustine's heretical past is recalled with so little censure—and no wonder. Properly Christianized, that Carthaginian circle would become the model for Augustine's monastic ideal—a community of friends engaged in mutual intellectual enrichment.

Though Augustine knew at least some of these people before he became a Manichean himself, one thing he would not have acquired from them—any sense of asceticism. Although Manicheism, like most late-antique systems of thought, made detachment from the body a condition of philosophical enlightenment, only the Elect embraced the full rigor of the teaching. "Hearers," like Augustine's friends, served the Elect without sharing their full vocation to otherworldly enlightenment. They resembled Christians who put off baptism.

It was the siren song of asceticism that pierced Augustine's soul when he read *Hortensius:* "I was elevated by that language, I was enkindled, I was aflame" (T 3.8). Cicero's dialogue, it is clear from the fragments preserved by Augustine and others, was a motivational exercise *(protrepticon)* urging the reader to pursue wisdom by renunciation of ambition and pleasure—and even of rhetoric (Grilli 24–25). Augustine would later quote from it the grim comparison of the soul's manacling to its body with the Etruscan pirates' torture of prisoners by strapping a dead corpse to them, buckled face to face (Grilli 52). The call to tame one's body as one would a wild horse had great appeal to Augustine—in theory. It was from this, his nineteenth year, that Augustine began aspiring to chastity—but not yet.

Cicero's dialogue embodied a paradox that Augustine would later live out himself, of the great rhetorician rhetorically dismissing rhetoric. Not the least part of its appeal to Augustine was no doubt the dialogue form. Unable to read Plato's more sinewy Socratic dialogues, Augustine loved Cicero's urbane tone, the high-minded exchange of views between interlocutors (exemplified in all Cicero's extant dialogues). Augustine's Manichean friends were, in that respect at least, Ciceronians. All Augustine's own earlier works would be dialogues, reflections of his view that all thought is an effort best pursued with others. Even when pastoral pressures made him give up the more leisurely dialogue form, there was a contrapuntal quality to his exchanges with a congregation in sermons, or his exchanges with God in prayer forms like *The Testimony*.

Given this immersion in the sophisticated conversation of Cicero, it is not surprising that Augustine was offended by the brutal directness of the Jewish Scriptures he turned to when impelled to seek wisdom by *Hortensius*. There was no dialoguing with Yahveh. He did not explain his demands to Job or Isaac. He was as imperious and punitive as Augustine's own father.

It is usually assumed that Augustine missed the verbal felicity of Ciceronian style in the African Latin of the translated Bible. What he actually says is that the scriptural approach *(modus)* fell below Cicero's seriousness (*dignitas*, T 3.9). The long passage that follows, rehearsing Manichean criticisms of the Bible, shows that it was the "childish" stories of the Old Testament that seemed unworthy of a classical seeker after lofty doctrine (T 3.13–18).

Manicheism, by contrast, offered a rational cosmology and a higher knowledge, preached by its martyr-founder, Mani. The sect did not suffer from the disadvantage Augustine felt in

Cicero—an ignorance of Christ's name, which still had some obscure hold on Augustine from his childhood. Manicheism was a Christian heresy (B and S 94–118). It treated Christ as the second person of its trinity—he was the Light, communicating the Father to those below. The third person was Mani himself, dispatched into the world by the Light. Manicheans believed that they contained exiled God-particles in them that had to be wrestled free from an enveloping and caliginous power of evil. This element of psychodrama fit Augustine's sense of his own internal contradictions. Manicheism gave Augustine categories for explaining himself to himself—much as Freud's hypostatized triad of superego, ego, and id served as a model for self-explanation to later generations. Manicheism gave Augustine his first experimental tools for psychological self-examination.

Though Augustine dates his "conversion" to Manicheism after his nineteenth year and the reading of *Hortensius*, and says he stayed with the sect for nine years, there is reason to suppose he omits a penumbra of engagement at the beginning as well as at the end. By the time Monnica came to stay with him in Carthage, he was already a Manichean, and it is hard to imagine that she had waited very long to see her grandson. Patrick had died in 371, Augustine's first year in Carthage. Monnica might have visited even before then, but her move to stay was delayed by a scruple about living under the same roof with a heretic (O'Donnell 2.198–99). It is significant that she does not have the same problem about living with Una. She consulted a bishop about her problem. It seems more likely that she returned to Thagaste, where her own bishop knew both her and her son—and only then moved in with Augustine in his establishment at Carthage.

This whole establishment, remember, was being subsidized by Romanian. When Augustine, at his patron's behest, returns to Thagaste as a teacher in 375, we are first informed that Romanian is a Manichean. It has often been assumed that Augustine converted him to his new faith. But this influence could have worked the other way. Romanian, who had made business contacts in the Western Empire, no doubt knew influential people in Carthage, to whom he would have recommended his young protégé. Some of these may have been the well-placed Manicheans who would become Augustine's patrons, in their turn, when he goes on to Rome. Manicheism had the glamour of fashion with an edge of danger (as a heresy, it was formally banned in the Christian Empire). Peter Brown (B and S 108–9) compares its appeal to that of "Bolshevism" in British universities of the 1920s. Romanian, with his cosmopolitan aspirations, may well have been a Manichean "fellow traveler" before Augustine came back to Thagaste, bubbling with a twenty-two-year-old's enthusiasm for his new faith. Romanian was not simply an intellectual reflection of his young protégé—as he would prove later on.

5. Thagaste: 374–376

WHEN, his own studies completed, Augustine began teaching in his hometown, he strove energetically to convert a Christian catechumen to Manicheism—and he succeeded. "I wrenched him from his faith" (*a fide deflexeram,* T 4.7). Now Amicus (as I shall call him, to avoid periphrases) became his closest friend, a replacement for the magic circle of young intellectuals he had left behind in Carthage. But when Amicus fell seriously ill, his Christian parents, fearing he might die, had him baptized while he was unconscious. When Amicus recovered consciousness, Augustine thought he could joke him out of what had been foisted on him—and felt aggrieved when Amicus dared to defy him, holding on to the faith that Augustine was ridiculing.

When Amicus did, in fact, die shortly after, Augustine plunged into a hysteria of grief. Half his own soul was gone—he would force himself to live only because half of Amicus' soul was in him. His sorrow was like a great external force alienating him from himself: "I was made a riddle to myself, and I asked my heart why, in its anguish, it was whirling me about" (T 4.9). The last part of that sentence is a quotation from a Psalm (41.6) that echoes God's rebuke to Cain for being angry when Abel's sacrifice was accepted: "Why, in your anguish, is your face contorted?" (Genesis 4.6). The echo is clear in the Latin of Augustine's Bible:

Quare tristis esset et quare conturbat me?
Quare tristis factus est et quare concidet facies tuus?

It is appropriate for Augustine to recall the story of Cain, whose inordinate grief God rebukes. Cain was guilty of mourning another's good fortune (*tristitia de alterius bonitate,* CG 15.71), which Augustine calls a great sin. God orders Cain to master his sorrow, but Cain, clinging to it, murders Abel. Then God casts Cain out of his homeland, driving him into the wilderness where Cain establishes the first city—from whose foundation Augustine dates the Earthly City that is opposed to the City of God.

What is unusual in Augustine's treatment of the Cain story is his long analysis of Cain's unmastered sorrow over God's approval of Abel. In the same way, Augustine is "dumbfounded and disoriented" *(stupefactus et turbatus)* when Amicus clings to the faith from which Augustine thought he had wrenched him. He tries again to convert him, with what he calls a crazed effort *(dementia mea)*. And just as God cast out Cain, he "cast my wretchedness far from You" (T 4.10), turning all things hateful to him. Augustine flees his hometown *(fugi de patria)* and returns to his heretical friends in what was for him, at this stage in life, the Earthly City par excellence. Once again, Genesis has provided a pattern for Augustine to read the deepest moral meaning of the Thagaste episode: his sorrow was world-darkening, earth-obliterating, self-annihilating because he had played the role of Cain to Amicus' Abel. Cain's Earthly City was founded in a state of perpetual war with itself, and Augustine says that he was his own divided kingdom after the death of Amicus: "I was restrained within my own unhappy territory, unable to live there or to get out" (T 4.12). This was the inescapable "homeland" he took with him as he left his native town.

6. Carthage: 376–383

RETURNED TO CARTHAGE, this time as teacher, not student, Augustine became a star in the galaxy of Manichean activists, winning successes in the "mad effort" that had failed with Amicus. As he says in *The Manicheans' "Two Souls"* (11): "Arguing with ill-prepared Christians, I usually won a self-defeating victory [*noxia victoria*]." As the winner in a public poetry contest, he was crowned by the scholarly proconsul Vindician, who favored him with good advice and friendship. In 380, he published his first book (now lost), *The Beautiful and the Appropriate*. The argument of the volume may be reflected in a later letter to a pagan (L 138.5):

> The beautiful, which we gaze on and praise for its own sake, has as its opposite the foul and ugly; while the appropriate, whose opposite is the inappropriate [*ineptum*], depends on some other it is paired with, and cannot be assessed in itself but only in connection with that other.

Though he says this book was still tainted with the Manichean notion that evil is a substance, he did not dedicate the book to any of his Manichean friends. Trying to advance himself outside his own circle, he addressed it to a distant rhetorician he had never met, Hierius (T 4.21–23). Despite his assurances to Romanian that he had returned to Carthage to acquire more learning for use in Thagaste, Augustine was clearly looking to farther horizons.

Though he was a skilled Manichean dialectician, his growing philosophical interests made him suspicious of the faith he defended against others so deftly. Manicheism had promised a *rational* alternative to scriptural myth, but his work in the "natural philosophers" (very likely Cicero's treatment of astrology-astronomy) made him doubt that the Manicheans' own cosmic myths accorded with the state of science in his day.

Manichean friends told Augustine his doubts about Manicheisan would be settled when its foremost African spokesman came to Carthage. This was Faustus, on whose name ("Blest") Augustine would play ironically. Despite a melodramatic asceticism (he had publicly renounced his parents), Faustus turned out to be a charismatic and engaging man, a spellbinding preacher, but no thinker. Augustine was inspired by his speaking skills but disappointed that he could not answer his deeper questions about Manichean truth. "What I had already been told he presented with a much smoother line—but how was serving things up in fancier cups going to ease my thirst?" (T 5.10). Though it had been reported that Faustus was an adept of the liberal arts, he had not even read the serious books Augustine was now sharing with his students (presumably Cicero's dialogues)—as he winningly admitted: "He was not entirely ignorant of his ignorance" (T 5.13). The two became friends. But Augustine, who had wanted to be the pupil, had turned into the teacher.

What makes that fact odd is that Augustine, a success on the hustings and a teacher to the teacher, was a failure in the classroom. His idea of polite exchange was left vulnerable to the student hooliganism Augustine had applauded, from the sidelines, when he consorted with the Subversives. Now he became the victim of such people: "Outsiders, looking almost crazed, barge shamelessly into classrooms and dispel any atmosphere for learning the teacher may have established" (T 5.14). Talk in the profession indicated that students in Rome were more docile, and Augustine used this as one of his excuses for slipping away from Carthage, without informing either his mother or his patron. Taking Una and Godsend with him, he was steering, as Aeneas had, for Rome.

II

ITALY (383–388)

1. Rome: 383–384

HIS VOYAGE TO ROME was Augustine's first harrowing experience of the sea. He would sail only one more time in his life—to get back to Africa, and to stay there. The sea, despite its beauty, was a terror to anyone venturing on it (Perler 57–81):

> What a theatrical show the sea puts on, with its shifting colors like veils—green (but many shades of green), or purple, or heaven-reflecting blue; and this show is more enthralling in a storm, a sight sweet to behold far off—but not to experience as a tossed and battered passenger (CG 22.24).

Mountains were symbols of God and his saints for Augustine. The sea was an image of death. When a Christian convert went down into the pool of baptism, he was *dying* into Christ, to be resurrected on the other side. Sailing the Mediterranean with Una and Godsend in 383 was going down into death, with little promise of life on the other side.

The Rome they reached was no longer the center of empire, even for the West. Now the center was wherever the emperor was (in 383, in Milan). But just *because* real power was gone, its simulacra were devotedly propped up—the old pagan apparatus of senators and offices and storied families. As Augustine would later wryly put it: "The Church extends throughout the world, Rome excepted" (L 36.4). Rome's senatorial class, touchy about its empty privilege, also gaped after fools to fill up its days. Ammianus Marcellinus, the greatest historian of the time, discovered to his chagrin how quickly Rome took up and dropped people of real talent (Ammianus, *History of Events* 14.6.12.18).

The Christian Church in Rome had to deal with this shallow society—which led to the rise of courtier-priests of the sort satirized by Saint Jerome (who was in Rome as a papal secretary when Augustine arrived, though they never met).

> A model for them all I can sketch for you at a stroke—this master pattern you will find repeated in others of the type: he makes sure to be up at dawn, to check the schedule of ladies he will be calling on; he ascertains the quickest routes to them, so he is all but in milady's bedchamber before she rises—the dirty old man [*senex importunus*]! His mouth, rude and impudent, is weaponed with ceaseless malice. . . . Go anywhere, he is there before you. Encounter any gossip, he either made it up or made it worse. (L 22.28)

One of these worldly priests was Jerome's own patron, Pope Damasus I, whose political canniness and personal hedonism anticipated the corruption of Renaissance popes—as did the violence of his election, in which 137 combatants were killed at what is now the Church of Santa Maria Maggiore.

At first, Augustine could view little of the Rome he had come to love in Virgil. While still suffering from his sea trip, he fell into a deeper illness. Luckily, his Manichean connections supplied him with a patron who took in the patient and his household, Una and Godsend, and their servants. Though Augustine, disillusioned with Manicheism, teased his host over some of the sect's farfetched tenets (T 5.19), he continued to profit by association with it. Manicheans, aware of their vulnerability should the government act on their outlaw status, cultivated important figures. More serious than Rome's native nobility, more disciplined than the populace, the Manicheans recruited people like Augustine.

They had reason to align themselves with the few serious pagans of the old school, who were also waging a war of nerves with the Christian imperial court in Milan. Such a pagan was Quintus Aurelius Symmachus, famous for his oratory. Symmachus belonged to a circle of scholars and poets which included commentators on Virgil like Servius and Macrobius. It is intriguing to reflect that Augustine might have met such celebrants of his favorite poet when he dealt with Symmachus—for Symmachus, by virtue of his rhetorical reputation, had the power to choose the court orator for the Emperor Valentinian, and he favored Augustine.

At the time when Augustine came to know him, Symmachus was not only a senator from a distinguished line; he had just been appointed prefect of the city of Rome, despite his clash with a former emperor over the removal of an altar of Victory from the Senate chamber. In his new office, he sent to Milan an eloquent plea to have the altar restored, as a symbol of Rome's antiquity and power. Milanese courtiers are said to have been moved by the way Symmachus imagined Rome herself pleading with the emperor to recognize her historic identity, "which gave the world its laws" (*Relatio* 3).

But the bishop of Milan, Ambrose, described what would happen if the emperor (a boy of thirteen) restored the altar: "Try coming to the church and you will find either no priest there or one who refuses you entry" (L 17.15). This famous struggle took place in the summer of 384, just when Augustine was winning his appointment from Symmachus. It was no doubt the first occasion for Augustine to acquire any real knowledge about the notoriously intransigent Ambrose, who over time would break three different emperors to his will. It was also the time when Augustine, having read himself away from Manicheism with Cicero's help, adopted Cicero's own skepticism of the New Academy. What prior opinion, then, would Augustine now form about Ambrose, who was a menace to his influential friends, both pagan and Manichean? Milan might be a dangerous place for him. But Augustine was determined to escape Rome, because his students—though not as unruly as those in Carthage—were deft at eluding payments to their teacher. After three bad experiences as a teacher—in Thagaste, Carthage, and Rome—Augustine was at last moving up, out of the "dominie" class. In fact, he sped to Milan in style, his office as court orator entitling him to ride by the imperial post, a privilege Constantine had been criticized for letting bishops enjoy (Ammianus, *History of Events* 21.16.18).

2. Milan: 384–386

IN MILAN, Augustine moved onto a higher social plateau. He would shortly have an establishment of some size—Una and his son, his mother and brother, two cousins, a body of students—as well as the slaves, stenographers, and copyists necessary for one of his station. A government career was beginning, with the prospect of marriage into wealth. Since marriage was primarily a property arrangement, and Monnica was still managing her dead husband's estate, she arranged the engagement to a Christian heiress not yet old enough to wed. (The legal marriage age for girls was twelve, so she was probably ten, since there was a delay of over a year.)

What, then, of Una? She went back to Africa, vowed to live a life of consecrated continence. Augustine describes his reaction to a wedding for which he showed a lack of enthusiasm (O'Donnell 3.10–11):

> Since she [Una] was an obstacle to my marriage, the woman I lived with for so long was torn out of my side. My heart, to which she had been grafted, was lacerated [*concisum*], wounded, shedding blood (T 6.25).

The language recalls what he had written on the death of Amicus (T 4.12):

> I held in my soul as it struggled against being held in, lacerated [*concisum*] as it was, and blood-smeared.

Why did he not simply marry Una? If she was of a lower class than his, an order of Constantine against class mixture forbade that. Besides, he could adopt Godsend and legitimize his birth in a proper marriage. More important, Augustine had, both in his Manichean days and under Cicero's exhortation in *Hortensius*, felt that a life of continence was the only discipline for a philosopher. Later, as a bishop, he would present laymen with the ideal of marriage where sex was indulged only for the begetting of heirs. He could not trust himself to stay continent with Una, where long habit held sway; but he no doubt fooled himself into thinking he could do that with the prepubescent bride promised him. But he soon found he could not remain celibate, even without the provocation of Una's presence—he took a "stopgap" mistress to tide him over until the marriage. It is characteristic that he did not resort to promiscuity, but to another sole concubine.

There is no way to excuse Augustine's treatment of Una—as his own later words about his situation show. But can we say that he "dismissed" her? She presumably had some say in the matter, and looked to her son's prospects as well as her own peace of soul. As a Catholic, she may not have been complacent about the paganism into which Augustine had descended by the time he reached Milan, and court life may not have appealed to her. The woman he loved for so long presumably had some will of her own, and the way he refused to name her may have honored her own wish. She would have been in her early forties when Augustine wrote *The Testimony*, ten years after this breakup, and living in the Catholic community of Africa, very likely in Thagaste, of which Augustine's friend Alypius was bishop at the time. At any rate, she would have remained in correspondence with Godsend.

When Augustine arrived in Milan, he paid a courtesy call on the great bishop of the city, Ambrose, and was greeted with cordiality. It is presumed that Augustine fell under the great man's influence. Late in his life, Augustine's belated expressions of reverence for him would contribute to that impression. But things written at the time of Augustine's stay in Milan and its vicinity give a very different picture. Then he writes that it was "cruel" of Ambrose not to have given him any guidance before his conversion (*Dialogue with Myself* 2.26). And even after his conversion, Augustine wrote to an intellectual friend that *their* life, unlike that of a bishop enmeshed in worldly affairs, would let them become detached enough from the world to "divinize" themselves (*deificari*, L 10.2). Augustine never corresponded with Ambrose after leaving Milan, never dedicated a work to him, and for a long time did not mention his name in his own writings. As O'Donnell writes to me, Augustine "only begins to use Ambrose in later life when he needs him" (as a fellow bishop whose example he can cite).

Augustine was not impressed by Ambrose's oratory—he said that Faustus, his glib Manichean friend, was a more winning preacher (T 5.23). Augustine's own sermons would be very different from Ambrose's. What is more, Augustine shows great reserve about the sensational miracles Ambrose was making public when Augustine arrived in Milan. The bishop was locked in a struggle for public control of Milan with the Arian empress, Justina, and he used the discovery of two martyrs' bodies (Gervasius and Protasius), with miraculous healings by the bodies, to whip up popular support for his position. Augustine mentions this momentous affair only as an afterthought, after telling the story of his conversion, as if to emphasize that he was not swayed by the dramatic events going on before he chose Catholicism. His cool account is very different from enthusiastic memories of this event during Augustine's later days as a bishop himself (O'Donnell 2.113).

We know that Augustine initially took a disapproving attitude toward miracles. He did not doubt that they occurred. But devils could work them, and God would not cheapen the main revelation, in Jesus' miraculous life and death, by competing with the devil in showmanship. Shortly before his baptism, the very year after Ambrose's miraculous coup, Augustine separated himself from those "daunted by hollow claims of the miraculous" (O 2.2.7). Three years later he spelled out his objections: "Miracles have not been allowed to stretch into our time, or the soul would always be looking for sensations, and the human race would grow jaded with their continual occurrence" (*True Religion* 47). Augustine may have been reserved about miracles because the Donatists in Africa had featured them in their cult of martyrs' shrines—a devotion Monnica shared.

The only audience Augustine reports with Ambrose (after his first courtesy call) before his conversion was to relay Monnica's questions about fasting in Milan (L 36.32, 54.3). When Augustine informed Ambrose of his conversion, it was in a letter sent from a villa he had retired to after his conversion (T 4.13). Ambrose, in reply, suggested he should read Isaiah—a prophet who totally baffled Augustine. Obviously Ambrose had not yet taught Augustine the symbolic approach to Scripture—that would come when he returned from the villa for his baptismal instruction.

If Ambrose did not play the leading role in Augustine's conversion, who did? Simplician—Ambrose's own mentor, who would also be his successor as bishop—helped in four crucial ways. First, he regularly received Augustine (CG 10.29), while Ambrose had put him off and never talked intimately (T 6.3). Simplician was a sympathetic interlocutor who "by asking questions like a student became the teacher of those he asked" (Gennadius 36). When Augustine corresponded with him later, calling him "Father" when they were both bishops, he said: "The heartfelt affection you show in your letter is not a new and untried vintage to me, but a familiar and treasured taste brought up from the cellars" (L 37.1).

A second service was Simplician's recommendation to read the letters of Paul, which engaged Augustine at levels Isaiah could not, at that time, reach. He was reading Paul on the day of his conversion.

A third service was the introduction of Augustine to a flourishing Christian Neoplatonism in Milan. Simplician had been a friend of Marius Victorinus, the translator of Plotinus. He had been Ambrose's mentor in the Greek philosophers. As the center of the Neoplatonist circle in Milan (O'Donnell 3.6), he was familiar with Mallius Theodore, to whom Augustine would dedicate one of his earliest works.

A last kindness he did Augustine was to tell him pointed

stories of others' conversions. Augustine recognized his strategy, but appreciated it: "After Simplician recounted the life of Victorinus, I was on fire to follow his example—which is why he had told me the story" (T 8.10). This was the first of a series of conversion accounts that form a kind of drumbeat leading up to Augustine's own conversion.

Restlessness with his professional duties increased as Augustine delved into Neoplatonist ideas and Saint Paul. His duty at court was to flatter—"The more my lies, the more I was applauded by the connoisseurs of lying" (T 6.9). He was disgusted at being "a phrase salesman" (*venditor verborum*, T 9.13). His health was deteriorating. It bewildered him that he could not give up his interim mistress, when the arguments for doing so seemed so clear.

On the day of his conversion, he began the great last struggle against grace by going into a garden with his old friend Alypius, where he plunged around in an agony of paralyzed will—just as he had flailed his limbs, in infancy, for lack of the words he needed to get what he wanted:

> Even while thrashing about with stymied effort, my will still had effect on my body—unlike the situation of those who have the will but not the bodily effect (because, perhaps, a limb they want to move is amputated, tied down, withered by a malady, or otherwise debilitated). No, when I tore my hair, pounded my head, laced fingers around my knee to hug it to me, I was accomplishing what the will told the body to do. The willing would not have been followed by this effect if my limbs were

pinned down, since here the effecting was a different thing from the willing. Yet I could *not* do what I far more ardently wanted to do, and which I should have been able to do at will, since what I wanted was, precisely, to will. Here the motion to be dictated was in the will itself, and simply to will were to do. Yet I could not. My body's limbs were moved by the soul's lightest volition, yet the soul did not respond to its own ardent willing, though this was its *own* will. (T 8.20)

In his agony, Augustine imagines a personified Self-Control (*Continentia*) islanded off from him in a place he fears to enter. She "reaches out hands of affection toward me, to receive and embrace me"—Virgil's image is vaguely present, of souls that yearn for a far shore, "stretching hands toward it" (*Aeneid* 6.314). The appearance of self-control is something that occurs "in my own heart, pitting myself against myself" (T 8.27).

Augustine then turns himself away from Alypius, to go deeper into his interior desert. He sits beneath a fig tree. Why stop to notice the particular species? Augustine is not at leisure, now of all times, for botanizing (Recherches 192). Pierre Courcelle (193) rightly argued that the tree is symbolic. He thinks the reference is primarily to Nathaniel under the fig tree at John 1.48. But after noticing all the other uses of Genesis in *The Testimony*, it is clear that we should think first of Adam's and Eve's inner division, which made them aware of their nakedness: "Puzzled at the insubordination of their bodies, a symbol of their own insubordination, [Adam and Eve] made aprons from the leaves of the fig tree" (CG 14.17). Before his fall, Adam wore the clothing (*indutamentum*) of grace. Afterward, his body was estranged from his will. Augustine, in the public baths with his father, had been clothed in the shame of Adam—but here, under the fig tree, he is about to put on the clothing of Christ.

Since Self-Control is a figure in Augustine's imagination, and the fig tree is symbolic, Courcelle argued that the child's voice Augustine now hears must also be a psychic event, not literal— Courcelle even used a rare textual variant to say the voice came from God's house (*divina domo*) not from a nearby house (*vicina domo*). But Augustine does not treat this like a metaphor or an interior event. He wonders if any child's game had the repeated chant *Tolle, lege.* Unable to think of one, he accepts the hint, understanding the words to mean "Pick up and read," and turns back to what he had been reading. A. Sizoo thinks one indication that the voice was real is the possibility that Augustine records it without really understanding it. Since *lege* often meant "select" rather than "read," he could have been repeating a harvesters' work chant, "Pick up and sort" (O'Donnell 3.63), an Italian chant not familiar to an African like Augustine.

In any event, Augustine instantly saw the meaning of the text he picked up under the voice's prodding: "Be clothed in Jesus Christ."

The very instant I finished that sentence, light was flooding my heart with assurance, and every shadow of doubt evanesced (T 8.29).

3. Cassiciacum: 386–387

As a convert, Augustine wanted to make a clean break with his past life. Una had already left. He laid plans to give up his court post, pleading ill health. He changed scene, going to a villa loaned him by a friend, Verecundus. He was not becoming just a Christian but a Christian ascetic. Verecundus regretted he could not join the company at the villa, since he was married. This elite Christian community would be made up of celibates (T 9.5).

There was a competitive note to this ascetical break with "lower" life. Though it was possible to be a Christian but not an ascetic, that did not fit late-antique views of what was proper for a *philosophical* adherent to any serious moral program. When Augustine had heard his last conversion story, just before he burst into the garden, he said to Alypius:

> What's the matter with us? Has it come to this—do you hear so?—that non-philosophers surge ahead and snatch at heaven, while we, with our cold learning—we, look at us, are stuck in the mire of our own flesh and blood? Just because they have got ahead, should we be ashamed to follow at *all* rather than shamed *at least* into following? (T 8.18)

This need for a strict renunciation in the pursuit of reason was part of what Peter Brown calls a Mediterranean-wide phenomenon. It shows up in the praise for pagan sages, as in Ammianus' tribute (5.4.2) to Julian the Apostate:

He was splendid, first of all, for his unvarying continence. After his wife's death [when Julian was twenty-five], all agree that he experienced no taint of sex, taking to heart what was said in Plato of the tragedian Sophocles, who, asked if he was still capable of intercourse in old age, said no, and added that it relieved him to escape that kind of love, as one flees from a crazed and ruthless despot.

Another sage, the emperor Marcus Aurelius, renounced sex (*Meditations* 2.15) as the mere "release of slime by rubbing a woman's innards." Augustine's attitude had, at this stage, as much to do with the purification of the mind in Neoplatonic terms as with anything specifically Christian.

Since Augustine and Alypius and Godsend all had to be back in Milan to begin their baptismal instruction by February of 387, they spent the early winter at Verecundus' villa—probably modern Cassago (A-L, "Cassiciacum," cols. 773–74). It was cold. We know this from a poem one of Augustine's students later wrote about the stay there (L 26.4):

> *Could Dawn, with happy chariot,*
> > *Wheel back to me the past,*
> *When we prolonged our wise retreat*
> > *'Neath Alpine shadows cast,*
> *No frost would now repel my feet*
> > *With firmness planted fast,*
> *No storms or winds beat off return*
> > *Of friendships meant to last.*

The villa was clearly a fine establishment, housing Augustine's company of ten, with its servants and stenographers. Augustine had not formally given up his court position, and the copyists would be kept very busy. No ancient author could be without his stenographers—Jerome (L 5.2) even took them with him into his desert hermitage.

Augustine was explosively productive during these months while he waited for induction into the Christian mysteries. This man, who had written only one book in his first thirty-two years, now wrote four dialogues in as many months, and planned an ambitious series on the whole circle of learning. It is as if he had been paralyzed by lack of an ordinating principle, the answer to previous philosophical doubts on the nature of mind and body, wisdom and God. He thought, now, that he had all the answers— he would soon learn better.

His model as a Christian author was the Neoplatonist Mallius Theodore, who had retired to Milan to escape political distractions from his philosophical work. Theodore wrote in the dialogue form, as we learn from Claudian's poetic tribute to Theodore's consulship (84–86):

> *Crabb'd Greek to Latin you transform,*
> *With skill at shaping urbane interchanges,*
> *A tapestry of truth from crossing strands.*

Theodore's later return to paganism would make Augustine revise his opinion of the man who had loaned him Neoplatonic books from his library. He is the nameless person "puffed with outsized self-inflation" at T 7.13 (O'Donnell 2.420). But Augustine's debt to him at the time of his conversion appears in the dialogue he dedicated to him, *Happiness in This Life* (1.45). There he refers to conversations with "our priest friend" about the nature of the soul—which has been taken as a reference to Ambrose. But we know Augustine had not *had* any philosophical conversations with Ambrose at this point, and Simplician was the center of the Neoplatonist group that included Theodore. "Our priest friend" (*noster sacerdos*) is a bit chummy for the aloof Ambrose, but not for the generous Simplician. Augustine's dedication shows how important Theodore was to him as he began his Christian studies:

> Since, my Theodore, I look only to you for what I need, impressed by your possession of it, consider what type of man is presented to you, what state I believe I am in, what kind of help I am sure you can give me. . . . I came to recognize, in the conversations about God held with our priest friend and you, that He is not to be considered as in any way corporeal. . . . After I read a few books of Plotinus, of whom you are a devotee, and tested them against the standard of the sacred writings, I was on fire. . . . So I beg you, by your own goodness, by your concern for others, by the linkage and interaction of our souls, to stretch out your hand to me—to love me and believe you are loved in return and held dear. If I beg this, I may, helped by my own poor effort, reach the happiness in this life that I suspect you have already gained. That you may know what I am doing, how I am conducting my friends to shelter, and that you may see in this my very soul (for I have no other means to reveal it to you), I thought I should address you and should dedicate in your name this early discourse, which I consider more

religious than my other ones and therefore worthy of you. Its subject is appropriate, since together we pondered the subject of happiness in this life, and I hold no gift of God could be greater than that. I am not abashed by your eloquence (why should that abash me which, without rivaling it, I honor?) nor by the loftiness of your position—however great it is, you discountenance it, knowing that only what one masters can turn a truly favorable countenance on one.

This is the most heartfelt tribute written at the actual time of his conversion. It ascribes more to Theodore's influence than to any other person's. It was composed, copied, and sent off quickly before Augustine's return to Milan, as if to keep up Augustine's presence in the Neoplatonic circle there. It also contained, in a long passage not quoted here, a brief summary of Augustine's intellectual development to that date—what has been called his first autobiography (O'Donnell 1.1i–1ii). He prefaced another of these dialogues (*Answer to the Skeptics*) with a similar sketch of his life, addressed to his African patron Romanian. He was clearly assessing his position by looking at how he had reached it, while at the same time creating the framework for his large future projects. As part of this reorientation of his whole life, he created a new form in one of his writings—his *Dialogue with Myself* (1.1):

Myself reflecting with myself for some time on various things, and persistently for many days quizzing myself over what I should seek, what avoid, I suddenly addressed myself—or some one did, outside me or inside I could not tell, though I am deeply concerned to find out.

Augustine invented the very term he used for this dialogue: *soliloquia,* "lone speakings," which is not what we mean by "soliloquy"—not, that is, a monologue, with oneself as the audience (Marcus Aurelius' address to himself is the normative example). There are *two* voices at work here, contrapuntally going at each other, with real differences and gropings: "Since *we* alone speak to ourselves, I prefer to call these exchanges—in writing them down—*soliloquia,* a neologism grating perhaps, but descriptive of what is going on" (2.14).

Augustine's intellectual need for the interplay of minds made him consider even friendship, at this point, as just a tool for finding truth (1.20):

> REASON: I ask you now why you want your friends at least to keep living, even when not actually living with you?
>
> AUGUSTINE: That we may together scrutinize our souls and God, so that whoever discovers anything can help the others to it more readily.
>
> REASON: But what if they do not join in this search?
>
> AUGUSTINE: I shall persuade them to.
>
> REASON: What if you cannot, either because they think they already possess the truth, or that it cannot be possessed, or because they are engaged in other business or pleasure?
>
> AUGUSTINE: I shall deal with them, and they with me, as best we can.

REASON: But what if their presence distracts you from your own search? Won't you take steps, or hope to, to be rid of them?

AUGUSTINE: You are right, I confess it.

REASON: So you do not want them to live or be with you for their own sake, but to help you find wisdom.

AUGUSTINE: I agree entirely.

This is the same attitude Augustine expresses in letters to friends in Milan during this retreat at Cassiciacum. To Hermogenian he wrote (L 1.1):

> I think we make enough concession to our times if any pure steam of Plotinus is channeled through dark and thorny tangles to refresh a few, rather than be loosed indiscriminately in the open, where its purity cannot be preserved from the random tramplings of cattle.

Augustine now misses his Neoplatonist friends in Milan the way he missed his Manichean friends in Carthage. But at Cassiciacum he feels he has a new mission, whereas in Thagaste he had no heart for his teaching after Amicus' death.

Life at Cassiciacum was not all high theorizing. Since he meant for his encyclopedic work to build up toward God from the basis of the liberal arts, Augustine continued to teach Virgil to the three prize pupils he had brought with him, adapting the poem to his Neoplatonist conception of the universe. He also used his pupils, friends, and relatives to conduct the conversations which were raw material for his rapidly assembled and edited dialogues—those on order in the universe, on happiness in this life, and on the refutation of skepticism.

His use of this material can be seen in the dialogue describing order in the universe. The work begins on a sleepless night when Augustine hears one pupil—Licentius from Thagaste, the son of Romanian—throw a shoe at a rat. Lying in the dark, Augustine wonders why sounds of a water channel near their bedroom gurgle to a stop, at times, then gush on again. The boy answers that leaves probably clog it until a buildup of water flushes them forward. Augustine congratulates him on his reasoning to a cause, and invites him to consider the ordering of all causes in philosophy. So excited does Licentius become at these new insights that he yodels an Ambrosian psalm while sitting at dawn in the outhouse. Monnica, whose singing he is imitating, thinks the song irreverent in that place. But Augustine says the place was *appropriate,* since the soul purges its darkness as the body does its waste (O 1.8).

These early dialogues bubble with a sense of creative beginnings. But Augustine's new life was not as securely under his control as he could at times imagine. In the dialogue with himself, Reason asks if Augustine is free of sexual temptations and he says yes (1.17). But the next day Reason asks if he was not tormented the night before by "imagined caresses soliciting you with the old bitter-sweetness" (1.25) and he must admit that he was. His earlier jauntiness was that of Hilaire Belloc with *his* troubled self:

> *I said to Heart "How goes it?"*
> *Heart replied:*
> *"Right as a ribstone pippin!"*
> *But it lied.*

4. Milan: 387

RETURNED TO MILAN by the beginning of Lent, Augustine was no doubt anxious to mix again with his fellow philosophers and to find out how his dialogues, sent back from Cassiciacum, had been received. While he was on a roll, he began an extension of the *Dialogues with Myself*. Now that he could talk again with Simplician and Theodore, he felt he could prove that the soul is immortal.

There was no scriptural commentary in the dialogues from Cassiciacum, a fact that has been used to indicate that Augustine's conversion was less to Christ than to Plotinus. But it would have been presumptuous for him to speak out on the faith before being instructed in its reserved mysteries, the *disciplina arcani*. And his real exposure to the symbolic reading of Scripture came with Ambrose's Lenten instruction to the candidates *(competentes)* for baptism—a disciplined course all Christians went through at the time. All through Lent, the candidates went unbathed, wore penitential hairskins, and were assigned a special place in church. We have two versions of the Ambrosian instruction on baptism—which traced prefigurings of this spiritual "bath" to Noah's flood, to the passage of the Red Sea, to healings at the pool of Siloam; to water that Moses sweetened, or water that floated Elijah's axe (*Sacraments* 2.2; *Mysteries* 1.3).

In this period, the candidates were given, by oral recitation, the Creed and the Lord's Prayer for memorizing. On Thursday of Holy Week they were allowed to bathe, then submitted to physical inspection (S 216.11). On the eve of Easter, they prayed through the night, renounced Satan at dawn, turned toward the sun, and were conducted to the octagonal pool we can still see, in a tunnel under the cathedral plaza of Milan (O'Donnell 3.106–7). There are few places in Europe more charged with historical significance than this baptistry where Ambrose, the creator of structured disciplines for the medieval Church, received as a Christian Augustine, the creator of the theology that would resound in that Church.

5. Ostia: 387

BAPTIZED IN THE SPRING, Augustine headed south in the summer, traveling now in humbler state than on his trip up, with a reduced company trying to reach Ostia before winter shut down the sea lanes back to Africa. But when they arrived there, they found the Mediterranean sealed off by war, not winter. The forces of both emperors, Eastern and Western, were finally arrayed against the usurper Maximus, whose court in Trier Ambrose had visited during Augustine's time in Milan.

While they were stranded in Ostia, Monnica was taken ill and died. I have not said much about Monnica so far because too much is often made of her role in Augustine's life. Rebecca West's indictment of her is well known:

> It was fortunate [for her] that in her religion she had a perfect and, indeed, noble instrument for obtaining her desire that her son should not become a man. . . . Very evidently Christianity

need not mean emasculation, but the long struggle of Augustine and Monica simply [meant] that in her case it did. Monica could have put him into the Church as into a cradle. He would then take vows of continence and avoid the puberty she detested . . . a son dead is as much a mother's undisputed property as a son not yet born.

Though Augustine is often presented as dependent on his mother, if not dominated by her, he was absent from her, during his grammatical studies in Madauros, from age twelve to sixteen. He lived in her town during his sixteenth year, but was at the estate of Romanian most of that time, and active sexually, probably with the woman who soon bore his son. When Monnica joined him in Carthage, after Patrick's death, he was not deterred from Manicheism by her abomination of it. He would long have an aversion from the very martyr cults and miracles that she was fond of. He lied to her when he ran off to Rome. Later, when she joined him in Milan to arrange a marriage, she traveled there with Augustine's brother and two cousins, the whole family sharing in his new fortune. In accounts of his conversion to Catholicism near the time of its occurrence, he gives credit to Neoplatonist Christians like Simplician and Theodore, not to her or to her hero, Ambrose. When Ambrose led resisting Catholics in prayer against the Arians' attempt to take over a church, Monnica was inside the church, "second to none in her concern and watchfulness," while Augustine stood outside "unsoftened as yet by the heat of Your spirit" (T 9.15).

Then why does Augustine spend so much of book 9 of *The*

Testimony on Monnica's biography? There are several reasons for this. The life of Monnica inserted in the Ostia section is like the other "potted" biography, that of Alypius (6.11–16)—elements of which Courcelle (31–32) thought preceded composition of *The Testimony,* since Paulinus of Nola had asked for a sketch of the man's life. There is an awkward "join" preceding the "biography" of Monnica that suggests it, too, might have had an earlier form. After saying he is rushed in his story and must omit much, Augustine breaks off the narrative form, only to say that he must not omit a sketch of Monnica. If the first eulogy of Alypius was meant for Paulinus of Nola, the story of Monnica may have been composed originally for the benefit of her children and grandchildren. The children stayed close to Augustine—Monnica's daughter was the head of the convent attached to his monastery, and one of her grandsons became a deacon in that monastery, where he had to divest himself of property held jointly with his sisters (S 356.3). Augustine would at any rate have consulted with his sister on their mother's life, and she may have furnished some details to the sketch. The sister had probably lived longer with her mother and closer to her in the women's quarters. Monnica might have confided more readily to a daughter the perils of, for instance, housekeeping where wine is concerned.

Augustine's own appreciation of his mother's worth seems to have come late—specifically at Cassiciacum. In earlier parts of *The Testimony* he had been harsh on Monnica when she lived only "on the outskirts" of God's favor (2.8; O'Donnell 2.308). But at Cassiciacum, in accordance with a Neoplatonic openness toward women as philosophers, Monnica joined in the philosophical discussions—at just the time when Augustine was judging all human relations in terms of their usefulness to the search for truth. Though Monnica was very likely illiterate (O'Donnell 3.115), she amazed her son by her shrewd insights. He laughed at her earthy response when she learned that Academics elaborately prove they cannot prove anything. "They have the falling sickness," she said (*Happiness* 16). She made an even sharper observation when a student denied Augustine's claim that the mind feeds on wisdom. She chimed in: "Didn't you yourself show us, just today, whence and where the mind is fed? After eating a bit, you said you had no idea what was being served, since you were thinking of something or other. Where was your mind when you were eating without knowing it?" (*Happiness* 8) Monnica had stumbled on one of Plotinus' proofs that the soul is detachable from the body: "You could list many worthy activities, theoretical and practical, which might as well not exist, so far as we are aware when we are thinking while doing them" (Plotinus, *The Nines* 1.4.10). Some of Monnica's remarks seemed almost oracular to Augustine, coming from one with no philosophical preparation. His own surprise, and her initial reluctance to participate, show that Monnica had not taken part in philosophical conversation before. Her son says, "I am daily struck anew by your natural ability" (O 2.45). Her piety he had long recognized, but not her natural acuteness (*ingenium*).

There is pathos in the fact that this belated recognition was followed so soon by her death. But before she died she shared with her son a conversation in Ostia that lifted them to a joint experience of what they were contemplating, carrying them above (and almost out of) their bodies. Augustine describes his inability to describe this moment (T 9.25) in a single long mounting and subsiding sentence (its climax I italicize):

If fleshly importuning were to fall silent, silent all shapes of earth, sea, air; silent the celestial poles; silent the soul, moving (oblivious of self) beyond the self; silent, as well, all dreams and shallow visions, all words and other signs, silent everything that passes away, all those things that say, if one listens, "We did not make ourselves, He made us who never passes away"; if, after saying this, they too were silent, though alerting us to hear the One who made them; and if He should speak, no longer through them but by Himself, for us to hear His word not as that is relayed by human tongue or angel's voice, not in cloudy thunder or confused mediation, but if we harkened to Him we love in other things *without* those other things (*as even now we strain upward and, in a mind's blink, touch the ageless wisdom that outlasts all things else*), and if this were made constant, all lesser vision falling away before it, so that this alone held the universe in its grip, in its enfoldment and its glad hidden depths, and eternal life resembled this moment of wisdom that we sigh to be losing—would that not be what is meant by the words "Enter the joy of your God"?—a joy that will be ours when?—only when all things rise (though not all are changed)?

That sentence takes the Ciceronian period to new heights. The step-by-step shooshing of the universe mounts by anaphora:

"Silent . . . silent . . ." The glimpse of "ageless wisdom" comes in a fleeting way, as a grammatical aside. Then the sentence falls off, fragmenting as the vision is dispersed, ending (in a dazed way) in questions.

Scholars have debated how far this "vision" fits Plotinian patterns for the ascent of the mind. What is interesting from a biographer's point of view is that the experience was communal, not a private ascent, and Monnica had not undergone the intellectual preparation of the liberal arts and abstract sciences that Augustine, in one of his moods, considered necessary for such an exercise. His experience was now at odds with his theory. The theory would have to be modified, if not abandoned. This is the true measure of Monnica's delayed impact on his thinking. In the overall scheme of *The Testimony*, the prayer at Ostia shows how the bond of company *(socialis necessitudo)* can lift one up to heaven—in contrast with the way it dragged Adam down when he joined Eve's motion away from God.

Monnica's other son, Navigius, was with her at the end—it was to him she confided her resignation of any hope to be buried with her husband in Africa (T 9.27). Part of the inscription over her tomb was found in 1945 by some boys playing by a church in Ostia. Godsend broke down at the death of his grandmother, but Augustine mastered his sorrow for his mother with Christian hope for her soul's future life. The passage stands in clear contrast with his earlier hysteria over the death of Amicus.

With the winter season now cutting off his return to Carthage, Augustine had no reason to stay in Ostia. He probably had influential Christian hosts there, but he would need libraries, better to be found in Rome, since he meant to keep up the furious pace of his writing.

6. Rome: 387–388

WHEN AUGUSTINE STAYED in Rome before, he was feted by Manichean and pagan notables, cultivating and being cultivated by Symmachus. This time he no doubt met Rome's Christian community. Pope Damasus had died, and his protégé Jerome had been driven out of town. Siricius, the new pope, had just been working with Ambrose to prevent a heresy trial of Priscillian by the usurper Maximus, so Milan ties would have brought Augustine to the pope's attention. Augustine was now the man who gave up a court orator's post to be baptized by Ambrose. But Augustine tells us nothing about his stay in Rome, whose glamour had dimmed with the renunciation of Virgil's world. Though he was often urged to return to Roman councils after he became a bishop in Africa, his dealings with the papacy would always be formal but distant.

Deprived of his large cast of characters from Cassiciacum, Augustine had to content himself with one interlocutor in his Roman dialogues, but this man, Evodius, was a curious and persistent questioner. He had belonged to the large network of imperial secret police, but he abandoned that life to follow Augustine from Milan to Africa (Mandouze 366–73). Augustine finished one dialogue (*How to Measure the Soul*) and began another (*Freedom of Choice*) in Rome, and wrote a treatise, *Catholic and Manichean Moral Systems*. He could have left Rome when spring opened the sea lanes, but he may have lingered, once he got into his work rhythms, until the onset of autumn threatened to close off the sea again. Reluctantly he went aboard a boat for the second and last time, going home.

III

AFRICA (388–430)

1. Thagaste: 388–390

SETTLED ON HIS FATHER'S PROPERTY in Thagaste, Augustine accepted for a while the duties of a decurion. New dialogues were written, but now his son was old enough (sixteen) to be an interlocutor—a brilliant one in *The Teacher*. By the time the dialogue was published, Godsend had died. Was his mother present when he died? It is overwhelmingly probable. She had gone back to Africa to live as a vowed Christian celibate. She must have returned to whatever was left of her family, which was probably in Thagaste. Vowed celibate women usually lived with their families in those days, unless the family provided money for life in a community. Augustine's sister would later be a nun within her brother's episcopal jurisdiction in Hippo, but she could well have been living a celibate widow's life in Thagaste before he went to Hippo. There is no evidence or probability that her son did not communicate with Una, and the boy who cried so at his grandmother's death would clearly want his own mother at his side when he was dying. Even if his death was a sudden one, she would have been nearby for his Christian funeral. The fact that

Augustine does not mention Una after his return to Africa could reflect as much her wish as his own. He did not mention his sister except when he had to exercise authority over her community. Augustine's ideal, even for married couples, was an affection without sex, and he had achieved enough self-control not to deny Una her maternal rights. He knew when he returned to Africa that he was returning to her region, perhaps even to her town.

It was clear in his earliest Christian writings that Augustine felt two duties incumbent on him—to expound the whole circle of knowledge in Christian terms, and to refute other schools, within Christianity or outside it. In pursuit of the first goal he began an ambitious treatise, *Music.* His other goal he had already pursued at Cassiciacum, where *Answer to Skeptics* renounced his own most recent errors, those of Cicero's Academics. But Manicheism, which had been a greater part of his past history, called for more thorough examination and refutation. He had already addressed Manichean ideas in his dialogues written at Cassiciacum and Rome. But now he finished one of the Roman works (*Free Choice*) and addressed Manichean dualism in *The Manicheans' "Two Souls."* Augustine had been a star disputant for the Manicheans, so he published these early works to clear his record. He began his first important treatment of Scripture to show that the "crude" Jewish account of creation makes more sense than the fanciful (indeed obscene) cosmogony of the Manicheans. This is Augustine's first attempt to deal with the Bible symbolically, and it is a bit tentative (*Genesis in Answer to the Manicheans*, 388–89).

Augustine was getting a new reputation, as a Christian apologist (it was now that his old pagan mentor from Madauros wrote him), so it was dangerous for him to travel outside Thagaste—churches of that day dragooned passing leaders into being their priests or bishops, and conscientious Christians had few defenses against this ordination by acclamation. Ambrose had been conscripted in this way when he was not even baptized. But Augustine thought it was safe for him to move to Hippo Regius, a seaport second only to Carthage, where he meant to set up a monastery with Evodius. That town seemed safe, since its bishop's chair was filled by the respected Valerius, who, by ecclesiastical law of the time, was the only one who could preach in his own diocese.

But Valerius was a Greek whose Latin was halting. He felt the inadequacy of his preaching, and wanted a man of more polished rhetoric. Who better than Augustine? Augustine fought the idea. He had been a Christian for such a short time. He pointed out his need to study the faith rather than preach it, his commitment to his monks in the new monastery, the fact that only bishops were allowed to preach. Valerius answered that Augustine could use the garden adjacent to his church as a monastery. He granted him time to prepare for his scriptural preaching, and absolved him from the ban on priests' preaching. Augustine felt obliged to give in. There went all his dreams of a lofty disengagement from the practical kind of life Ambrose was leading.

2. Hippo: Ministry (391–396)

THE PERIOD GIVEN Augustine to prepare preceded the Lenten season of 391, and his schematic treatment of the early Psalms (P 1–32) probably reflects the kind of study he first engaged in. Since the Psalms were used extensively in the liturgy, both in readings and in songs, Augustine tried to establish the *layers* of prayer in these poems. Often "David" is speaking prophetically in Christ's person. But since Christ's body is the Church, all Christians can participate in Christ's sufferings and glory, just as all of Israel was given voice in David's song. A rich weave of the historical and the personal, of inner voice and public harmony, is established, a continual ascent through the layered text:

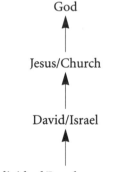

God

↑

Jesus/Church

↑

David/Israel

↑

Individual/Local community

All these levels are active at once, but with shifting emphases according to the exact verse. Whenever the Psalmist is a sinner, that is David speaking for his fellow penitents. Whenever the

Psalmist is sinless, innocent, unjustly treated, or judging others, that is Jesus speaking of his suffering and triumphs. Christians should identify with David by their sins, or with Christ by his grace.

This approach to the Psalms set the pattern for many kinds of sermons. The complexity does not come so much from stretched analogies and learned ingenuity, as with Ambrose's sermons, but from a need to make the text fit the community's psychological participation in it. Augustine was learning to bring his high-flown theoretical aspirations down to the level of ordinary people. The man who was going to write only for "the few" now found himself addressing "the many" several times each week. Eventually he would see that this "fleshing" of ethereal abstraction reenacted the Word that became incarnate in Jesus:

> The word in my mind exists before it is put into language. I search for the right sound to carry it abroad. I need a way for it to reach you without leaving me. And even now you are hearing what I have in my heart, and it is in yours. It is in both of us, and you are now possessing it without my losing it. And just as my word had to take on sound in order to be heard, so God's word took on flesh in order to be seen. (S 225.3)

Even when he stopped writing dialogues, he was still teaching (and learning) by interchange with others. He taught catechism with the same alertness to each flicker of attention that he had shown with his students at Cassiciacum. Here is how he coaches other teachers in the skills demanded:

It is hard to speak on to the end of what you planned to say if you see a listener is not responding—he might be afraid, in such sacred matters, to differ in words or bodily reaction, or he may not grasp or approve what he is being told. Since we cannot see into his mind, we must use words to get a response from that mind, to lure it from its hiding place. . . . We should wake him up, mentally, with some catchy witticism (fitted to the subject), or bring up something odd and astonishing, perhaps something scary and depressing, preferably having to do with him personally, so self-interest will stimulate him. Yet use no severity; ease him into candor. (*Instruction* 1.18.19)

The need for catchy witticisms to hold an audience's interest has subjected Augustine's sermons to criticism from Gibbon and others. He uses puns, wordplay, jingles, all kinds of verbal fireworks, to drive home his point. He can deploy rhyming tags, like the modern preacher Jesse Jackson: "Faith must *hold* what it cannot yet *behold*" (S 230.7). Or, to show that the faithful, as the body of Christ, should care for their own members: "Where the sliver rends [one's foot], the whole back bends" (S 162.A.5). Or, to study God's revelation through Peter, a humble worker: "The fisherman's scope is the rhetorician's hope" (S 43.6). The military profession is not evil in itself, though soldiers often are: "The damage is not done by militia-ness but by maliciousness" (S 302.15).

His vivid and earthy comparisons give us what Erich Auerbach called *sermo humilis* at its most pungent. As dung heaped on a field brings forth shining wheat, so penance heaped on the soul brings forth virtue (S 254.2). The Cross was a mousetrap, with the body of Christ as the bait, to trap the devil into loss of his dominion over man (S 263.2, 257.5). Humor is used to ridicule those who would take pride in vows of poverty—they are asking to be called "Sir Bum" (*Domine Pauper,* S 14.4). His effort at vividness can be almost grotesque. To give force to John the Baptist's words "He [Christ] must go higher, I lower" (John 3.30), he notes that the manner of each man's death illustrates the words: Christ went higher on the Cross and John was made shorter when he lost his head (S 380.8).

That Augustine took pride in his own virtuosity as a preacher can be seen in the advice he gave to the clergy he was training, telling them that even plainness can pack a wallop:

> Often even the plainest prose—if it takes up intricate problems and resolves them with an unexpected approach, or draws shrewd insights from unexpected sources (as from some cave or other) and brings them to the light; or if it refutes an opponent, proving that false which seemed invincibly true; doing all this with a certain economy, unstudied and, as it were, spontaneous; with rhythm of phrase not showy but dictated, almost inevitably, by the very things at issue—all this can provoke such applause that the prose hardly seems plain. What else can explain such applause but men's delight in seeing truth so presented, so protected, so impregnable? Thus even in the plain style your teacher-preacher [*doctor et dictor*] should take steps to be heard not only with understanding but with pleasure and assent. (*Instruction* 4.56)

Some try to excuse Augustine's pyrotechnical displays by saying he had to "talk down" to his African audience. But we find him using the same devices—puns, jingles, alliteration—in his more theoretical or intimate works. It is in *The Testimony* (7.26) that he mocks his pagan philosophizing as a demonstration that he was "not expert but expiring" *(non peritus sed periturus)*. Augustine meant to learn as well as teach when he spoke with fellow believers. His quick responsiveness to an audience's mood, his improvisation when a text was not working, his bracing rhythms, rhetorical questions, repeated pleas that people listen closely— his almost comic efforts at clarity—show how engaged he was with his listeners: "As far as I can, I'm turning myself inside out for you" (S 120.2).

The bond of union Augustine forged with his community appears from passages like this:

> If it becomes boring to repeat the same things to beginners, we should put ourselves in their affectionate brother's place, or their mother's or father's. Then such will be our empathy with what they are feeling that what is said will become new to us again. The effect of this sympathy is so great that when listeners are moved as we speak, we enter into each other's reactions, as the hearers speak in us and we learn in them what we were teaching. Isn't that what happens when we show others beautiful scenes which we have often gone past with a careless glance, but which give us fresh joy as we share others' joy on first seeing them? And the intensity of this experience is the greater, the closer we are to each other. The more, by the bond of love, we enter into each other's mind, the more even old things become new for us again. (*Instruction* 17)

The importance of sympathy in teaching and ministry was always in Augustine's mind: "One becomes sick oneself, to minister to the sick, not with any false claim to having the same fever but by considering, with an attitude of sympathy, how one would want to be treated if he were the sick one" (L 40.4).

Any account of Augustine's ministry should begin with his preaching, since that is how he first made himself useful, indeed indispensable, to Bishop Valerius. To have given Augustine, a mere priest, the privilege of preaching in Hippo was unusual enough. Valerius went even further when the pan-African council of bishops met at Hippo in 393, just after Augustine's ordination. Valerius secured the bishops' agreement to have a priest address them on the subject "Faith and Creed." The basic nature of that speech, which has survived, shows how badly the African clergy were in need of instruction. Luckily the primate of Carthage, Bishop Aurelius, was a reformer with visionary plans for the African Church. He and Augustine struck up a partnership that would remake the face of African Christianity over the next several decades. Augustine knew the size of the task before them, since he had recently confided to his own bishop: "How can I castigate wrongdoing or deception [in lay Christians] when these faults are far worse in our own ranks than among the people generally?" (L 22.2). Augustine would train in his monastery many of the bishops Aurelius helped place in key dioceses over the coming years.

The coordination of the reform effort comes out in a letter jointly written by Augustine and Alypius to Aurelius in Carthage.

They thank him for making it a general practice for priests, as well as bishops, to preach. The level of learning and discipline in the three hundred African bishops had sunk so low that young, better-trained voices had to be brought forward. The two younger men present this development with shrewdly voiced humility: "Let sacred ants bustle along their route, let sacred bees do their fragrant work" (L 41.1).

Augustine knew that the effort at cleansing the Church had to have two aspects—internal improvement and disarming of the omnipresent Donatists. The Donatists were heirs to African Christianity's finest and darkest hours, during Diocletian's Great Persecution of 303–305. Donatists had tenacious memories, with an abiding scorn for the quislings in that time of trial, who were called "Scripture betrayers" since the clever tactic of the persecutors was to get Christians to be "handers-over" (*traditores*) of their sacred books. Donatists—named for Donatus, a martyr-hero of the resistance to compromise—refused to accept the *traditores* back into communion, or else demanded a new baptism (a rite that had been approved by Africa's great martyr-bishop, Cyprian, in the third century). A *traditor* bishop was readmitted by the Donatists as a layman, if at all.

The Donatists' insistence on fidelity to death made the martyr's shrine the center of their cult. Pilgrims to these shrines included a violent wing of the Donatist movement, one ridiculed by its enemies as "hut people," *circum-celliones.* They apparently recruited from or mingled with immigrant workers at transient lodgings (A-L, "Circumcelliones," cols. 930–36). These extremists called themselves the Lord's Athletes (*Agonistici*). Their chant

Laus Deo became a war cry, and the clubs they carried were known as "Israels" for smiting foes. They kept the impure from their sacred places (the same tombs we have heard Augustine's mentor in Madauros ridicule for the uncouth names of those buried there). They trafficked in relics and in miracles worked by them. They ranged the countryside courting martyrdom themselves, making a circuit of the shrines much as later pilgrims would journey for their souls' redemption to the Holy Land. For them, Africa was the Holy Land.

Though Augustine would do much to publicize these extremes of the Donatist movement, it was not merely a mob religion. Peter Brown has argued that Frend overdid the rural nature of Donatism (R and S 237–59, 279–300, 325–38). It had, until repression closed them, important urban churches. Augustine could hear the chants from their Hippo basilica as he was celebrating mass at his own altar (L 29.11). Bishop Aurelius at Carthage was paired against a great Donatist organizer and reformer in the Donatist bishop of that city, Parmenian. Augustine admired the lives of some Donatist bishops and learned much from their greatest scholar, Tyconius. The Donatists and Catholics were each other's resented twin brothers. They matched up church for church, bishop for bishop—when finally forced to a conference together in 411, 284 Donatist bishops were able to attend, and 286 Catholics. Brent Shaw has argued that the contrast between Donatists and Catholics was not rural versus urban but indigenous versus universal. Donatism was the African church. Catholicism the imperial one.

Though Augustine's personal experience had been a matter of

sifting philosophic positions (Manichean, Academic, Neoplaton-ist), he could not have grown up in Africa without rubbing up against Donatist-Catholic tensions, always ready to erupt in city streets like the jostling of Montagues with Capulets. His distaste for Ambrose's use of martyrs and miracles in the theatrical presen-tation of the martyred bodies of Gervasius and Protasius probably came from his knowledge of the shrines cultivated by the Do-natists, who camped out near them.

His first instinct in dealing with Donatists was to cool off the family feud by an amnesty. Both sides had their grievances, de-voutly nurtured. Donatists recalled the use of imperial force to suppress them (at Catholic instigation) under Count Macarius in 347, when Donatus was killed in an assault on his basilica in Carthage. The Catholics had circumcellian atrocities to recount. As a newly ordained priest, Augustine tried to make overtures to Donatist bishops in and around Hippo:

> Let us take out of play the unproductive charges that the masses on both sides hurl at each other. If you do not bring up the Macarian period, I pass over the wild "hut people." Say that the latter have nothing to do with you, nor the former with me. The Lord's threshing floor is not yet winnowed, there is bound to be chaff among us both—let us pray only, and take steps, that together we may be His wheat. (L 25.6)

It is a plea he will return to often at this stage of the quarrel. He writes another Donatist bishop:

I ask you what sense do these old quarrels make for us? The profound resentment of unbending partisans has kept the wounds of our congregations open for far too long, wounds whose deadened flesh has become insensate, so we feel no need for the doctor. (L 33.5)

Augustine's own family, he tells us, was divided between Donatists and Catholics (L 52.4), a common situation:

Husbands and wives, peaceful in bed, part company at Christ's altar. They call on him to grant peace but cannot come to Him together. Children and parents are at home in the same house but not in the same church. They are willing to come to terms over property benefits, but clash about Christ's benefit for us. Slave and master rend the God who became a slave in order to give us mastery by His service. Your adherents come to our courts, ours to yours. We accept all cases, we want none to take offense. Can Christ alone take offense when we tear Him member from member? (L 33.5)

He assures a Donatist brother-bishop, "God knows I shall take no steps that anyone be forced into joining with Catholics against his will" (L 34.1). He asks only for a hearing, and says the Donatists can set their own terms for public discussion (L 33.4). If the Donatists think he is too skilled at controversy, they can deal with another Catholic bishop (L 34.5–6).

Augustine would like to stress similarities, not differences: "We call on the same God, believe in the same Christ, hear the same gospel, sing the same psalm, respond with the same Amen, chant the same Alleluia, celebrate the same Easter" (P 54.16). He placed great hope in public discussion—that had been a Manichean procedure he was skilled at. Early in his priesthood he had confounded a former Manichean colleague, Fortunatus, in public debates. Fortunatus eventually became a Catholic.

But most Donatists could not be lured into such intellectual combat. The emphasis on keeping their faith pure made them take very seriously scriptural admonitions to shun unbelievers. They would not even greet Catholics (a harsh rebuff in the African world), much less join them in debate. In Augustine's own Hippo, Donatist bakers refused to sell bread to Catholics (*Answer to Petilian's Letter* 2.184). Rebuffed in his efforts at mediation, Augustine fired long-range ammunition against the Donatists in what Peter Brown has called a journalistic campaign, satirizing and stigmatizing the enemy down the street. Augustine could be slashing, as when he he turned the Donatists' pride in their localism against them: "The clouds above proclaim that the Church is rising everywhere in the world, while these frogs grunt from their little pond: 'Christians? None but us' " (P 95.11). But Augustine was responding in kind to the programmatic vilification of Donatists. Even Frend, sympathetic to the Donatists, admits that "their sermons consisted of Scriptural texts coupled with invective against their enemies"—what Yves Congar called a "mélange de violence et d'onction."

Things took a harsher turn when some Donatists sided with Gildo, an African general who rebelled against Rome. The suppression of Gildo involved the suppression of some Donatists, and Augustine, who once had agreed to forget the hut people, was by now harping on them in a stream of polemics.

Yet Augustine had to recognize that Donatists, by their very fanaticism, were often purer in practice of their religion than much of the laxer Catholic community. It has rightly been said of the Donatists: "Perhaps no other movement in the history of the church with the possible exception of New England Puritanism had such a low tolerance of human sinfulness." Augustine had to make his own community a model of the Christian life that others could aspire to. He provoked a showdown with Catholic laxity in 395, determined to break through the hardened customs of his auditors. He describes in a letter to Alypius (who was already a bishop in Thagaste) how carefully he stage-managed the affair. Bishop Valerius had ordered his community not to indulge in the customary drunken festival on the feast of Hippo's first bishop-martyr, Saint Leontius. The community openly resented this interference with a beloved holiday, and seemed determined to resist it.

Augustine took up the cause two days before Saint Leontius' Day, on the eve of the Ascension. He lined up a powerful set of scriptural readings to be pronounced by the lectors as he marshaled them to a climactic denunciation of drunkenness in church ceremony. He was disappointed at the poor showing that day, but he soon learned, through the tight little community's network of gossip, that the people's anger at Valerius had been turned against him.

He upped the ante the next day, with a new barrage of readings and an emotional plea that the people not imperil his soul through its responsibility for them.

> This rebuke was delivered with all the fire and skill our Teacher and Leader could lend me against so great and dangerous an offense. I did not move them to tears by weeping myself. But when the words were finished, *their* tears overcame me and I could not refrain from weeping myself.

But once again Augustine picked up rebellious comments, and he was braced for the worst on the next day, the actual time set for feasting. He prepared a sermon on the doom of those who would not repent, and was ready at its conclusion to rend his garments and depart from so sinful a people.

His determination must have become evident by now, since the ringleaders of the opposition came to him to say they would abandon their planned celebration. The sermon was changed to explain why past festivities could be justified historically (as the excesses of a young church, just emerged from persecution, with a flood of untrained new Christians coming into it). The celebration in the church extended past noon with spontaneous songs and readings. Augustine was experiencing the emotional eruptions he had considered demagogic in Ambrose.

That afternoon, the celebration of vespers was again crowded with people. Bishop Valerius gestured for Augustine to speak, though the latter was anxious to retire now and let the bishop's authority conclude the day. But then he heard noisy celebrations from the Donatist church, and he could not refrain from boasting that Catholics were now the ascetical party. When Valerius and Augustine left, people stayed on singing and praying till dark. An emotional running engagement with an initially refractory and finally tamed congregation had gone on for fifty hours. It was like the great preaching triumphs of a Savonarola or Whitefield, turning a whole people around. As O'Donnell says, this was Augustine's "own local triumph, and the making of his reputation as a figure of authority at Hippo" (2.336).

Valerius now had to worry that this wondrous reformer would be snatched up by any diocese where a bishopric came open. So, outdoing the audacity with which he had made him a preacher, Valerius pleaded with the primate in Carthage that Hippo be granted the rare privilege of having *two* bishops, to nail Augustine down to his place. Aurelius got other bishops to go along with this—they were unaware that this kind of arrangement had been forbidden by the Council of Nicaea. In 395, Augustine was consecrated a bishop, at age forty-one, four years after becoming a priest and eight years after his baptism.

The new bishop realized it was not enough to satirize Donatist excesses or to outdo them in ascetical discipline. He needed a counter-ecclesiology to show why Donatists' purism, their hope for a community admitting only saints, was not scripturally warranted. He performed a raid on the Donatists' own greatest thinker, Tyconius—a man who had been too open toward the corrupt world for the Donatist leader Parmenian, who engineered his excommunication by a Donatist council shortly before Augustine's return to Africa from Italy. Tyconius never came over to the Catholics, despite his repudiation by the Donatists. Augustine calls him a man "of a conflicted spirit" (*absurdissimi cordis, Instruction* 3.42). He was "to so bad a cause untiringly true" (*Letter to Catholics* 1).

The strategic thinking behind Augustine's use of Tyconius is hinted at in the letter he wrote, along with Alypius, coordinating a reform program with Aurelius. After asking that Aurelius send them copies of the new sermons being preached by priests, Augustine adds a personal note: "Nor am I neglecting what you asked for. And I await your decision on Tyconius' *Seven Rules (or Keys)*, as I have frequently told you in my letters." This was not a matter of mere intellectual curiosity, as the tactical tenor of the whole letter shows. Augustine had been urging a decision (*quid tibi videatur*) on the use of Tyconius, a heretic, to confute heretics. Aurelius might well hesitate to have Augustine praise a Donatist as "a man gifted with penetrating intelligence and persuasive rhetoric" (*Answer to Parmenian's Letter* 1.1).

But Augustine was not merely using Tyconius as a Trojan horse into the enemy's camp. He was deeply impressed by Tyconius and indebted to him in every area of his thought. Tyconius supplied him with what Ambrose could not—a set of standards for keeping the symbolic interpretation of Scripture from random ingenuities. Tyconius' *Book of Standards* was the first Western examination of the exegetical method in terms of systematic use and the disciplining of abuses. Frend no doubt exaggerates, but in the right direction, when he says (205): "With Ambrose Tyconius may perhaps have shared the honor of finally winning Augustine from Mani to Christ."

Tyconius' rules for reading Scripture stressed the importance of distinguishing when a text is spoken of Christ in Himself or Christ in His body of believers—just the distinction that Augustine observed in preaching from the Psalms. It is probably a distinction he had learned from Tyconius, whose condemnation by the Manicheans before his death c. 390 made his a cause célèbre at the very time Augustine was beginning his ministry. The fact that Augustine had frequently (*saepe*) been writing to Aurelius about the use of Tyconius before 397 shows he had long been familiar with him.

What Tyconius gave Augustine for particular use against his fellow Donatists was a theology of the Church that admitted it was made up of saints and sinners, who could not be sundered until the final judgment. Here Tyconius used a parable that would be the touchstone of Augustine's thought on the Church, and the core around which the whole *City of God* would later be formed—the Matthew text (3.30) that says wheat and weeds must grow together until the final (and sole) separation. Others had used this text, on both sides of the Donatist debate. But none had given it the depth of analysis that Tyconius did.

As early as 393, Augustine was using the Matthew text to instruct Catholics on their own claims to a biblical view of the Church. Parmenian had made popular chants a form of Donatist instruction. So Augustine composed a *Chant Answering the Donatists*, 297 verses of accentual verse with mnemonic devices, jingles, a refrain. This is far from the quantitative verse Augustine had grown up loving in Virgil; but it hammers home the new ecclesiology, using the wheat-and-weeds parable, and parables with a similar point in Matthew's Gospel—the net that contains a mingled catch (13.47–48), the chaff that cannot be separated from the wheat till they have been harvested together (3.12).

Collect the wheat at world's loss,
　　Winnowed then by Christ's cross. (181)

The winnowing comes after reaping,
　　Meanwhile falsehoods we are weeping. (185–86)

See church as net, and world as sea—
　　Saints, sinners in net mingled be.
We sail on to the end of time,
　　Then doom is fixed, what's yours, what's mine. (10–12)

Augustine was willing to use every tool, from polite diplomacy to slangy verse, in order to bring peace to the divided churches of Africa. But he was not willing, yet, to use force. This was not because of the first concepts that spring, somewhat anachronistically, to our mind—separation of church and state, tolerance, freedom of inquiry. That was not the language of the fourth century. What troubled Augustine was a concern very personal with him. State coercion might force a person to lie, claiming a belief he did not have. Augustine was an absolutist on the need for truth. Lying was always a sin, but lying about religious belief was blasphemous sin, and people should not be impelled toward that.

Augustine's attitude toward feigned religious positions is demonstrated in a correspondence, taken up at this time, that became a comedy of errors. Saint Jerome had written, in his commentary on Saint Paul's Letter to the Galatians (2.11–14) that

Saints Paul and Peter could not really disagree, so they had only feigned disagreement. The idea that deception can serve religion shocked Augustine so deeply that he wrote a letter of protest to Jerome, then residing in Bethlehem. The couriers never reached Jerome, but copies of the letter circulated in Rome, a place Jerome felt (rightly) was filled with his enemies. Not getting any answer from Jerome, Augustine sat down in 395 to thrash out the problem of lying for a good cause. The result was a treatise (*Deception*) in which, as Sissela Bok puts it, Augustine "left no room for justifiable falsehood." He considers the *worst* lie to be that which religion deploys for its own advance. This passage (*Deception* 17) goes straight to Jerome's use of Paul:

> From religious instruction and from all who in any way speak where that instruction is given or accepted, every vestige of deception must be absolutely excluded. Nor should it be held that any possible excuse can be found for deception in such matters.

Two decades later, when Augustine wrote another treatise, *Forswearing Deception*, it was because a correspondent asked if one could lie to a heretic in order to trick him into confessing his heresy. Again Augustine voiced his profound revulsion at any claim that God's cause can be advanced with lies. He held that Christians could not lie under persecution, and Donatists should not be compelled to lie by forced conversion.

Augustine had no way of knowing, when he addressed Jerome, that that brilliant writer and scholar was an enthusiastic liar about himself and a grim traducer of others. Jerome had been driven out of almost every place he lived in, including his birthplace. It was as rare for him to keep a friend as for Augustine to lose one. Thus, when Augustine kept writing to Jerome for an answer on the Galatians problem, the testy grump of Bethlehem snarled back:

> Some of my friends, themselves carriers of Christ (there are many such here in Jerusalem and the Holy Land), have hinted to me that you had as your secret aim to win a vulgar esteem, from the praise of sycophants, by your manipulation of me— to let everyone know that you issued a challenge and I shrank from it; that you, the scholar, wrote letters, while I, the dunce, sat silent; that someone had at last been found to shut up my babbling. Well, I admit I was wary of answering Your Eminence since I was not sure your letter was authentic and that the sword might not (as the saying of one of our lowly folk has it) be smeared with honey. Also, I did not want to be dismissive of a bishop of our faith [Jerome was just a priest] and to answer a correcting letter with correction—all the more because I discerned heretical things in it. . . . So if you want to bully with your learning, or show it off, find some youngsters, bright and well-born (Rome boasts many such, I hear), who have the means and will to submit to the labor of debating a bishop on the Scriptures. I am retired from my soldiering, and I should just applaud your prowess not wrestle it with my withered limbs. [Jerome was seven years older than Augustine at the most, and perhaps as little as three years older.] (L 72.2–3)

Augustine answered with deft self-deprecation:

Your letter makes me feel like the upstart Dares as Entellus began to pummel him into dizzy spins with his hail-storm slashing blows (L 73.1).

Augustine is recalling the way a retired elder came back to put a youngster in his place at *Aeneid* 5.458–60.

> *As hail drums on a resonating roof,*
> *So he rained thundrous blows from either hand*
> *To pummel Dares into dizzy spins.*

Yet Augustine persisted on the point of truthfulness that mattered to him most—and Jerome muttered back inconclusively (L 70). Augustine had also raised, more tentatively, a point that Jerome rightly dismissed. For pastoral reasons, Augustine did not want to make too many drastic changes in the Latin Bible his audience was familiar with—for one thing, the Donatists might say the Church was "cooking the books" for its own purposes by changing Scripture. We see how, even today, more scholarly translations upset people who think their faith is being tampered with. So Augustine suggested that Jerome should revise the Latin, when that made it conform with the Greek translation of the Old Testament, instead of starting all over from the Hebrew. If Jerome had been certain that Augustine was ignorant not only of Hebrew but of Greek as well, he would have been even more sarcastic in his rhetoric:

> You—placed, young as you are, on a bishop's pinnacle—may teach the nations, decorating Roman homes with your exotic

African produce, while I am content with whispers to a lowly hearer or reader in my monastery corner (L 75.22).

Though Augustine later made common cause with Jerome, it is clear that these two men were temperamentally incapable of understanding each other. Pious legend, with the help of forged letters, would later tell of a final friendship between them, and of mystical communings at Jerome's death—a legend brilliantly painted by Carpaccio, Botticelli, and others. About the only way Jerome could get lasting friends was posthumously.

3. Hippo: Implosion (397–409)

IN 397, WHEN AUGUSTINE had been two years a bishop and six years a priest, he was summoned deeper into the consequences of his own thinking, deeper into himself. That is when he began *The Testimony*, an intimate form of writing set apart from the sermons, pamphlets, and letters his duties drew from him in a constant stream. The explosion of writing that had occurred after his conversion in 387 was accompanied by a desire to catapult himself up out of his past, in a Neoplatonic ascent to God. Beginning in 397, there was an implosion of his mind, down into himself, back into his past, as the place where God could be found. His own mystery was an echo of God's; and God was hiding in the vaster areas he felt opening "within"—*intus*, the key word of his current quest: "You were inside me, I outside me" (*intus eras et ego foris*, T 10.39). God was "deeper in me than I am in me" (*inte-*

rior intimo meo, T 3.11). So, with a spelunker's hardy nerve, Augustine lowered himself into himself:

> I venture over the lawns and spacious structures of memory, where treasures are stored—all the images conveyed there by any of our senses, and, moreover, all the ideas derived by expanding, contracting, or otherwise manipulating the images; everything ticketed, here, and stored for preservation (everything that has not been blotted out, in the interval, and buried in oblivion). Some things, summoned, are instantly delivered up, though others require a longer search, to be drawn from recesses less penetrable. And, all the while, jumbled memories flirt out on their own, interrupting the search for what we want, pestering: "Wasn't it us you were seeking?" My heart strenuously waves these things off from my memory's gaze until the dim thing sought arrives at last, fresh from depths. Yet other things are brought up easily, in proper sequence, from beginning to end, and laid back in the same order, recallable at will—which happens whenever I recite a passage by heart. (T 10.13)

This recitation from memory is a key experience for Augustine, since it gives him an analogy for God's creation of time out of eternity. The poem stored up in Augustine's memory has no temporal extension. It acquires that only as he sounds out its syllables, in a long chain for a long poem, a shorter span for a short one. So the world and all its works resided in God's eternity, and only occurred in time when *His* Word articulated the eternal design in a sequence of created ages.

Even the recitation of a poem reveals a trace of the Trinity in man (God's image):

Say I am about to recite a psalm. Before I start, my anticipation includes the psalm in its entirety, but as I recite it, whatever I have gone over, detaching it from anticipation, is retained by memory. So my ongoing act is tugged [*distenditur*] between the memory of what I just said and the anticipation of what I am just about to say, though I am immediately engaged in the *present* transit from what *was* coming to what *is* past. As this activity works itself out, anticipation dwindles as memory expands, until anticipation is canceled and the whole transaction is lodged in memory. And what happens with the whole psalm is equally what happens with each verse of it, each syllable— and with the whole long liturgy of which the psalm may be a part, or with the whole of any man's life, whose parts are his own acts, or with the whole world, whose parts are the acts of men. (T 11.38)

Vladimir Nabokov had obviously been reading Augustine when he made Humbert Humbert describe his own self-awareness as "a continual spanning [*distentio*] of two points, the storable future and the stored past" (*Lolita,* Section 26). Time is a shuttling of the future into the past, moving through an immeasurable point. "If we could suppose some particle of time which could not be divided into a smaller particle, that alone deserves to be called the present, yet it is snatched from the future and flits into the past without any slightest time of its own—if it lasted, it could be divided into part-future and part-past. So there is no 'present' as such." (T 11.20) And yet, paradoxically, we know the past only as a *present* memory and the future only as a *present* anticipation. There is, then, no real present and nothing *but* a real present. The mind brokers this odd interplay of times in a no-time.

Philosophers, including Ludwig Wittgenstein, say Augustine fails to solve the very problem he poses. Bertrand Russell finds that old standby of Augustinian criticism, sex, at the root of the difficulty:

> St. Augustine, whose absorption in the sense of sin led him to excessive subjectivity was content to substitute subjective time for the time of history and physics.

But Augustine was not trying to solve an abstract philosophical problem. He was exploring his own mystery as a reflection of God's mystery. In his own activities he finds himself both trapped in time, tugged in its dialectic of future and past, and somehow outside time, holding the future and the past in *present* acts of anticipation or memory—that is why he scrambles his tenses so artfully in the paragraph above ("the *present* transit from what *was* coming to what *is* past"). Augustine did not delve into his soul to find sin. He went there to find God—and that is where he *did* find Him. This turned these great middle years of his life into a torrent of discoveries, the excitement of which pulses through *The Testimony*.

Three things gave focus to his thought in this period—the human mind's mystery, God's creation of time out of eternity, and God's triune nature. The themes were continually interwoven, yet he devoted separate books to each of the three, books composed in overlapping periods. He began *The Testimony* in 397 and was perhaps still polishing it in 401. He began *The Trinity* in 400 and *First Meanings in Genesis* in 401—they were finished, respectively, in 416 and 415. All these books, despite their primary focus, treat all three of Augustine's great aspects of these years—in fact, *The Testimony* can only be understood in terms of these three concerns.

The problem of *The Testimony*'s unity is often approached from the wrong end. It is customary to say that Augustine wrote ten books of autobiography and appended to them three books of very different sorts—one of philosophy (book 11, on time and memory), one of Scripture study (book 12, on Genesis), and one of theology (book 13, on the Trinity). O'Donnell (3.251) rightly points out that these final books are themselves a trinity, each devoted primarily to a different person of the divine Trinity (11 on the Father's creation of time, 12 on the Word's articulation of the world, 13 on the Spirit as the love that binds all three Persons).

These were Augustine's real concerns as the fourth century turned to the fifth. So the real question is: why did he prefix the ten narrative books to the three devoted to his central concerns? We have already seen part of the answer. Augustine was *already* discussing Genesis, from a personal viewpoint, when he wrote of the pear theft in conjunction with Adam's sin, of the public baths in conjunction with Adam's nakedness, of his friend's death in conjunction with Cain's anguish. He was also treating the Trinity, as O'Donnell extensively proves, throughout the first nine books. Patterns of three (the three temptations, the three measures of reality, the three cardinal virtues) run all through the theologi-cally structured account of Augustine's life—as does the cognate number six. Book 12 treats the six stages of history as reflecting the six days of creation, and Augustine refers to his own life in the six-ages-of-man scheme. Six is a "created" extension of three, since it is a sum of its first three integers (one + two + three). Theology, not psychology, determines what Augustine includes or excludes *throughout* the book.

Another aspect of Augustine's new insight is even more im-portant, not only to the structure of *The Testimony*, but to the reason for the first ten books' existence. Albrecht Dihle has ar-gued persuasively that Augustine in this period created a whole new concept of the will. In his Neoplatonist days he held that the intellect is man's highest faculty, that which lifts humans above animals partway toward the angels. But, of course, Satan had a high angelic intellect above any man's. What he lacked was love, a faculty destroyed by prideful regard for oneself. The self-imprisoning will was something Augustine had been studying in 394–395 when, with the help of Tyconius' guidelines, he wrote on the Pauline Epistles—Romans and Galatians. His trinitarian the-ology would be built on an understanding of God's free will as "loving love" (*amans amorem*): "Love is the act of a lover *and* the love given the loved person. It is a trinity: the lover, the loved per-son, and love itself" (Trin 8.14). The faculty of will had been comparatively neglected in classical thought, which tended to treat wrongdoing as error (the sinner just misconceives his real interests). Augustine would change that. Dihle goes so far as to say that "the notion of will, as it is used as a tool of analysis and description in many philosophical doctrines from the early Scholastics to Schopenhauer and Nietzsche, was invented by St. Augustine."

This change in Augustine's values led him to reassess the understanding of his own past. Dialogues written at the time of his conversion present his development as almost entirely intellectual—a journey from one school of thought to another, using his mind to purify his life by a progressively higher consideration of the divine. When he writes *The Testimony*, he looks back on that sequence to find a deeper struggle going on, between pride and divine grace. Now the great tug-of-war in the garden is seen in Pauline terms, as the incursion of a power (grace) that man cannot summon on his own.

People are quite right to see a contrast between Augustine's self-presentation at the time of his conversion and his description of the same events over a decade later. Augustine shows in his *Reconsiderations* that he came to see the dialogues as inadequate and immature. *The Testimony* reassesses the story in a considered and scriptural way. The *real* story was an *inner* drama of which Augustine himself was not fully conscious. *The Testimony* plays down the role of philosophers like Mallius Theodore in changing Augustine's mind. The role of his mother's prayers is now taken more seriously. Even Ambrose is beginning to look better in Augustine's eyes, as the providential occasion for his acceptance of grace. The wisdom for judging all those human transactions flows backward, in *The Testimony*, from its "high ground" of the last three books.

There is, of course, no misrepresentation in Augustine's

changed version of his life. We have seen that of all deceptions he
most abominated any deception used for a religious purpose. He
had come to see his early understanding of his conversion as inadequate, one that stood in need of correction. That is why we
have the first ten books, whose energy in pursuit of a truth still
being absorbed gives them their immediacy. He is now seeing,
late though it may be (*sero*), what he only partially saw at the
time. The books are a perfect example of his new concept, the
present memory of the *past*. For Augustine, the recovered self is a
transcended self, which is how he can remember his sinning
self without sinning again by the memory. The mere tug-of-war
that time imposes (*distentio animi*) is turned into a continuity
over time (*extentio animi*) and a medium of self-regulation
through time (*intentio animi*)—another of those triads Augustine finds everywhere in himself:

> Your right hand upholds me, my Lord, in Your Son, who re-
> joins dividedness in Your oneness, that through Him I may
> comprehend my Comprehender, that from days of prior dis-
> persion I may collect myself into identity, putting the old be-
> hind me, yet not tugged toward future temporal things; rather,
> reaching toward [*extentus*] higher things. I go, not in a tugged-
> about way but in a steering way [*non secundum distentionem
> sed secundum intentionem*], to the reward of Your call from
> heaven. (T 11.39)

This collection of a self from past self-dispersion is what *The Testimony* enacts.

Augustine's new emphasis on the will does not mean that he

undestimates the mind—as we can see by the treatment of light in another of this period's great works, *First Meanings in Genesis.* This book is usually translated *The Literal Meaning of Genesis.* But that is far from Augustine's view of what he is explaining. He was no literalist in the fundamentalist sense. The gibe Clarence Darrow used against William Jennings Bryan—how could God create light on the first day when He did not create the sun until the fourth day?—was already used by Augustine to show that "light" and "days" in Genesis, in a "literal" sense, make no sense (G 1.17). Although Scripture has many layers of meanings, it also has *first* meanings, the ones principally intended by God, if only we can find them (Augustine often admits that he cannot find the first meaning for this or that verse). Since God's creative act is single and simultaneous, the six "days" articulate categories for *our* mind, and the light of the first day is the light of intelligibility for us to understand the categories. That light creates the answering intelligences of the angels. The blaze of their minds' response to God makes up the "days" as they see the beauty of His creation.

Then what are the nights? They cannot be physical occurrences, Augustine says dismissively, except to "flat-earthers," since the sun is always shining somewhere on the round earth (1.21). If the days are the divine likeness of intellection turned back toward God, nights symbolize the angels' limited knowledge when turned toward limited creation (1.43). The same light illumines even *our* limited knowledge as men, since God is always creating light in us by the never-ceasing act of our creation as rational beings. It is the "light that enlightens every man coming into the world"

(John 1.9). As the Psalmist says, "By your light we shall see light" (35.9). Augustine's concept of illumination means that God, as the source of all good, directly illumines us by the natural working of the intelligence He is continually creating. That is why He is "deeper in me than I am in me" (T 3.11), not only by the action of His supernatural grace but by the natural action of our own minds. We know God by the mystery of *our* intellect that reveals *His* mystery. That is the "day" God creates at Genesis 1.1. The *first* meaning of light is the Intelligibility that creates its receptacle as intellect. For Augustine personally, it was the flood of illumination he was experiencing in these breakthrough years.

In the third of his central masterpieces, Augustine again searches deep into himself to find the Trinity. The three aspects of memory-time (anticipation of the future, present attention, past memory) have the dynamic found in the soul's three faculties of will (toward action), intellect (of articulated reality), and memory (establishing identity). In this we see a dim reflection of benevolent will (the Spirit of Love), articulating order (the Word as Son), and self-recognition (the Father as origin):

> If we take ourselves to the inmost memory of the mind, by which it "calls itself to mind," and to the inmost intellect by which it understands what is called, and to the inmost will by which it loves what is called, we find that the three are invariably conjoined, conjoined from the time they came into existence, whether this was reflected on or not. It appears that this image of threeness is a oneness of memory—yet since no word can be accepted as true without reflection (we think as we speak, if only by an interior word not formed in any known

language), it is best to understand this as a trinity of memory, intellect, and will. (Trin 14.10)

This controlling analogue generates, in the book's long exercises of self-reflection, a whole series of confessedly inadequate images of God—where even the unknowability of oneself is derived from the ineffability of divine reality. The mind is a perpetual wonder to Augustine: "I do not know how to explain the odd fact that we do not know we know certain things" (*nescio quo . . . scire nescimus*, 14.9). And so are the words that the mind generates to deal with itself:

To handle words with words is to interweave them—like interlaced fingers: rubbing them together makes it hard to tell, except by each finger on its own, which is doing the itching and which the scratching (*Teacher* 14).

In this magical decade-and-a-little-more, Augustine developed all his most characteristic themes—time, memory, the inner dynamic of the self, the inner dynamic of God, the continual activity of God in the soul, first by ongoing creation and then by regeneration in grace. If we had none of Augustine's writings except from this period, they would be enough to ensure his status as one of the greatest thinkers in history. And one of the greatest writers. His style underwent a deepening in this period—one seen in the sighing replications of *The Testimony*, based on psalm patterns. The jazzy style and pyrotechnics of his sermons are now tamed and put in service to the longer arcs of thought spun in his treatises. Words respond to the gentlest turns of his increasingly subtle inquiries. We can watch the drama of ideas as they emerge and struggle in his mind. The text does not deliver us a product, but calls us into a process.

4. Hippo: Power Relations (410–417)

WHEN THE VISIGOTH leader Alaric captured the city of Rome in 410, a shock ran through the entire empire. Jerome wrote from Bethlehem: "Rome, capturer of the world, fell captive" (L 127.12). Though Alaric was a Christian (Arian) taking a Christian (Catholic) city, there was an ominous feeling that the world structure built by pagan Rome was disintegrating. Pagans claimed that Christians had destroyed the greatest human achievement ever contrived. Christians themselves, who had boasted that they saved whatever was good in ancient civilization, lifting it to new heights, now suffered a crisis of confidence. Catholics in and around Rome, uncertain of their fate under the Arians, poured into Africa, bringing tales of breakdown at the center of things (though both Christian emperors, of the East and of the West, still ruled, from their courts at Ravenna and Constantinople). A need for new discipline and toughness was felt, to which Augustine would respond, showing a dark side to his teaching on the importance of the human will.

While working on his three concurrent masterpieces at the beginning of the fifth century, Augustine had kept at his ordinary tasks—preaching, church reform (at frequent councils called by Aurelius in Carthage), and endless controversy with Donatists.

Though Catholics were still asking for public discussion as late as 403, an increase in Donatist violence led Stilicho—the imperial minister at Ravenna who had been harsh on the Donatists since their participation in Gildo's African revolt—to issue an Edict of Unity in 405, punishing Donatists under the long-existing laws against heretics. Augustine had misgivings about Stilicho's policy, but he enforced it in Hippo, and his own attitude toward disorder and dissent was hardening.

A symptomatic after-effect of Rome's fall was the Pinian affair (411) in Hippo. The highborn and wealthy Albina, a devout Christian, left Italy with her daughter Melania and her son-in-law Pinian. They went to an estate in Thagaste, Augustine's birthplace, where his friend Alypius was now bishop. Albina wrote to Augustine hoping he would someday visit them. Since Augustine said he was unable to leave his church, Alypius took the three famous people to Hippo—where the congregation tried to induct the wealthy Christian celebrity Pinian as their priest, though Augustine had pledged that the visitor would not be pressured into that service. When Alypius tried to get his endangered guest out of the church, the people charged him with keeping Pinian to himself so he could control his vast holdings for Thagaste. Augustine told his congregation it could gain Pinian as priest only by losing him as its bishop. But his congregation was frenzied and he could not quiet it. He withdrew to the apse and drew its curtain shut. Pinian sent word to him that he would not be ordained, but that he would take an oath to live in Hippo and not to accept ordination elsewhere. After tense negotiations over the terms, Pinian took this oath—only to skip town the next day

(L 126). Alypius took the view that a coerced oath is not binding, but Augustine's strict line on deception, *especially* where religion was involved, made him write that Pinian must return to Hippo according to his word (L 125). Hard feelings all around were later assuaged, and Pinian went to the Holy Land, where he became a monk and Melania became an abbess. The story shows what a touchy matter it was for Augustine to control his volatile community, even after that early showdown over the drunken celebration of a martyr's day.

Augustine was a judge over property and other disputes, since the empire "farmed out" as much of its administrative tasks as it could, letting bishops hold ecclesiastical courts even for civil matters. These hearings were a time-consuming distraction for Augustine, but he felt obliged to conduct them daily (VDM 259–65), since they gave him a chance to teach moral principles of equity and social concord. They also let him set an example of leniency in punishment, something he was always preaching to Roman officials. He was, he hoped, saving some people from the imperial judges, of whom he had a low opinion: "Ignorance in the judge is often doom to the defendant" (CG 19.6).

Augustine's court arbitrations show how little we can speak of church and state as separate things in the fifth century. From the very time when Constantine recognized Christianity, the emperor held jurisdiction over matters of faith, calling councils, declaring what was orthodox, outlawing heresy. Arian emperors suppressed Catholic views, ousting Athanasius and other orthodox trinitarians from their episcopal chairs—and Catholic emperors did the same to Arians. It was generally conceded that heresy could be punished with fines, confiscation, torture, and even death. Ambrose denied churches to Arians and synagogues to Jews. Even the Donatists did not challenge the laws against heresy—they simply denied that they applied to schismatics like themselves, people who differed from orthodoxy only on matters of church discipline. There was religious intolerance all around. It was not an aberration but the norm.

Augustine, however, supplied something that *was* new—a *theory* of suppression. It is a sign of the general acceptance of religious intolerance that no one had felt the need to justify it. Augustine, as Peter Brown points out, formed his theory as a matter of conscience, trying to reconcile his own acts with his own values. In the process he mitigated what were harsher measures, gave a didactic restriction to repression, and opposed torture or execution. But by putting his theory in express terms, he bequeathed a dangerous legacy to later ages. He, not others, is looked back on as the patron of repression—not Ambrose, for instance, who practised it far more extensively and heavy-handedly than Augustine ever dreamed of doing.

Earlier, Augustine had drawn on the Donatist Tyconius to defeat Donatist ecclesiology. Now he made an even more daring raid on the enemy's arsenal. Tyconius, in his treatment of Saint Paul's claim that grace abrogated the Jewish Law, had said that the Law was prescriptive, not redemptive, that it convicted men of sin but could not save them from it. Then what use was the Law in God's providential guidance of the Jewish people? It was like a pedagogue, forcing the child to go to school, where he could freely learn once he had been compelled to attend.

At that time, the Law was compelling [*cogebat*] people to faith. Faith would not otherwise have sought out grace, since sin's power would not have been clear.

We had to submit to the Law as our pedagogue who would compel [*cogeret*] us to embrace faith, compel [*cogeret*] us to Christ.

Providence increased and guarded the seed of Abraham that, from the austerity and fear imposed by the Law, many might be compelled [*compellerenter*] toward faith.

In Luke's parable of a wedding banquet (14.23), when invited guests do not show up, the master sends people into hedges and byways with the order: "Compel them to come in." Augustine used both verbs available in his versions of Luke—*coge intrare* (the African texts) and *compelle intrare* (the Vulgate). Augustine brought Tyconius' argument to the interpretation of that verse. Perhaps as early as 411, Augustine was preaching:

Let the heretics be drawn from the hedges, be extracted from the thorns. Stuck in the hedges, they do not want to be compelled [*cogi*]: "We will enter when we want to." But that is not the Lord's command. He said, "Compel them to come in." Use compulsion outside, so freedom can arise once they are inside. (S 112.8)

Brown recognizes that this was not just an excuse cooked up as a cover for what was happening. Wrong by later and better standards, Augustine's view nonetheless grew out of deepening convictions at several levels. For one thing, it reflected his stress on the importance of the will. Faith was not simply an intellectual process. The will must be summoned. But the power of habit, of *consuetudo,* can imprison the will. The network of habit indurated by the Donatists' feuds with Catholics made it impossible for them to meet with, debate, or listen to inherited foes. To break that deadlock would be, Augustine came to hope, a way of freeing Donatists to hear, at least, what had been sealed out of their consciousness. That is why Augustine stressed that the aim should be use of the laws for teaching the truth in love. The pedagogue's aim is "*instruction* under hardship" (*per molestias eruditio,* P 118.2). Forcing people to listen is only the first step in a *discipline* that stresses that word's etymology (*disciplina* from *discere,* to learn). Stubbornness and pride can create the kind of *socialis necessitudo,* the partnership in crime, that Augustine felt in his own youthful gang of the pear theft, or in Adam's solidarity with Eve. That bond must be broken to get a fair hearing from its prisoners.

Brown points out that few inquisitors are going to have Augustine's scruples and restraint; but Augustine came close to finding his ideal partner in Marcellinus, the tribune sent by the emperor Honorius to deal with Donatist resistance in 410. In response to heightened violence from the hut people, Catholics had gone to Ravenna asking Honorius to deny violent people the sanctuary given them by Donatist bishops.

Marcellinus was given the task of bringing together the whole body of Catholic and Donatist bishops in a Confrontation (*Conlatio*) to decide which side, if either, was heretical under the old laws. Though a Catholic himself, Marcellinus conducted this great showdown—held at the Baths of Gargillius in Carthage—in an exemplary way. "Patient under every test, he moderated the debates with authority, never rude but also never weak, with a lawyerly respect for the rules and for everyone's rights" (Monceaux 4.423).

Before the Confrontation, Marcellinus restored to Donatists the churches taken from them by the Edict of Unity. He guaranteed their bishops personal immunity while traveling to and from the meeting. Augustine, writing for the Catholic bishops, entered into the spirit of Marcellinus' proceedings. He issued a public agreement that Catholics would surrender their churches and offices if the ruling went against them—but that they would let Donatists keep their churches and offices if they abided by a judgment forcing them to join the Catholics (L 128).

The Donatists knew that, no matter how fairly conducted, the laws under which the Confrontation would be heard were already tilted against them. If they had to attend, they would turn out as many of their bishops as possible. Even though their numbers were depleted when they excommunicated their own dissidents, the "Maximianists," they wanted to show that they still made up roughly half of the population, more than could be oppressed. They tried to keep down the number of Catholic bishops on the scene by challenging the way some (including Augustine) had been consecrated. The Donatists showed up as a body well before the opening date, while Catholics straggled in and had to make a last-minute effort to equal the Donatists. The final number of those attending—which did not count those absent for reasons of age, illness, or distance—was 284 Donatist bishops, 286 Catholics.

Marcellinus laid down rules meant to seem fair as well as efficient (though Brent Shaw argues that the hearing was, of its very nature, rigged). To guarantee equal speaking rights, and prevent a general shouting, Marcellinus told each side to choose seven speakers, backed by seven advisers or researchers, and four men to make sure an accurate record was being kept. But on the opening day, when the Catholics sent the required team of eighteen, the Donatists arrived en masse, demanding that all be admitted. Once inside, they refused to be seated with sinners, so Marcellinus, a layman who did not want to be seated while bishops stood, had to conduct the whole day's proceedings on his feet. Then the Donatists demanded that every bishop be credentialed individually, proving that he authentically represented his local church, with rights of challenge from the opposite side. Some bishops proved to be illiterate (Monceaux 4.423). The Donatists demanded that records not be taken in shorthand, so they could see instantly, on the spot, if the proceedings were being accurately reported.

Tensions ran high. Augustine had preached in Carthage beforehand that Catholics should stay far away from the baths, so as not to be drawn into scufflings (S 358.6). The Catholic bishop from Macomades tried to defuse hostility with "gossipy interventions, recognizing and greeting everyone from Numidia" (Monceaux 4.424).

When the debate on substance finally began, the origins of the *traditor* controversy were explored. The Catholics had documents to show that some condemned as *traditores* had been cleared—Augustine had supplied some of these to the other side ahead of time (L 88). But the Donatists seemed to have no strategy but obstruction. Frend (279) describes their disarray:

> In contrast to the Catholics, who leave the impression of abiding by a well-thought-out scheme of attack, the Donatists prepared their case indifferently. They even included documents which could help their opponents, and, as already mentioned, they seem to have been unable to decide until the last moment whether to include their [proconsular] primate [Primian] among the delegates chosen for debate. Perhaps they felt that Primian was too vulnerable on the Maximianist issue [as the suppressor of another religious body]—perhaps there were other grounds [old age].

The skill of Augustine, the organizing discipline of Bishop Aurelius, and the trained lawyer's talent of Alypius—these were a hard combination for the Donatists to match (Mandouze 671–84). It is fascinating to read the stenographic account of the debates. When Augustine was giving his argument for a mixed Church, where wheat and weeds grow together, Emeritus of Caesarea, the best exponent of the Donatist position, showered him with Scripture passages setting an evil world (*mundus*) against God. Augustine, with his total command of the Bible, was ready with answering *mundus* citations: "that *the world* may believe" (John 17.20), "that *the world* would be saved" (John 3.17), "reconciling *the world* to Himself" (2 Corinthians 5.19). Frustrated, the Donatists tried to shout him down. "As he was trying to speak, he was heckled" (*streperetur*). Alypius struck in: "Let the record show they are interrupting him."

Paul Monceaux (4.425) reads the musical "score" of the proceedings this way:

> There is enjoyment to be found in the plot-twists of this imposing pageant—in the strategies, for instance, of either side, the clear and concerted plan of the Catholics, the inventiveness of the Donatist obstructors. Above all, the mobile features are limned of some great orators. In the schismatic ranks, the headlong Petilian of Constantine, imaginative, rasping, unbending, slippery, almost always eloquent—or Emeritus of Caesarea, unbending too, but highminded, often wordy and drawn-out, but at times sparkling and witty. On the Catholic side, in a circle of outstanding speakers, all of these his friends, the clear winner of the Confrontation was Augustine, the verbal technician of his age, impassioned, wary, discriminating, and deadly.

After the third plenary session broke up on June 8, Marcellinus did not go to bed before making his decision, which was formalized in an edict on June 26—the heretic laws were said to apply to the Donatists, who thus lost their churches, were forbidden to hold meetings, and were fined for not attending Catholic church. Enforcement, as Brown notes (R and S 309–16, 335–36), was bound to be uneven, depending on the willingness of local landowners to make trouble for themselves by cooperating with the decree. Fines were even harder to collect than taxes (that perennial problem of the empire). Ordinary people would not be pursued. Leaders were more vulnerable—they lost their church holdings and their power to protect the hut people (who responded with another wave of suicides). But a leading Donatist bishop, Gaudentius, held his church for nine years at least, and perhaps for his whole life, despite a blistering attack on him by Augustine. Violent resistance to Marcellinus' edict led to the prolongation of terrorism. One of Augustine's priests had his eye put out and a finger cut off. Another was murdered. Enforcement of the law outside major cities was virtually impossible. According to Frend (299), "In the countryside, archaeologists have yet to find clear evidence for the transformation of a Donatist church into a Catholic one."

Augustine was preaching concord to the Donatists:

> Nothing in you do we hate, nothing detest, nothing denounce, nothing condemn, except human error. We repeat, we detest human error from regard for divine truth, but we acknowledge all of God's graces [sacraments] in you, while whatever in you has gone astray we would correct. . . . The stray is the one I would seek out, find, admonish, approach, take by hand, and lead, correcting the deserter not defacing his divine image. (S 359.5)

He told Catholics not to crow over Donatists like victors (L 78.8). Any Donatist bishop who joined the Church could keep his office, even though that violated the rule against two bishops in a single town. He personally would alternate service in his basilica with the Donatist bishop of Hippo.

When the murderers of his priest confessed, Augustine showed what he meant by discipline as a *teaching* instrument. He begged Marcellinus not to execute, maim, or flog the men (the customary Roman penalties).

> We agree that criminals should lose the freedom to commit more crimes. But we hope it does not go beyond this—that, while retaining life and sound limbs, they should be compelled by law away from their mad instability toward a sober steadiness, and be assigned some useful labor to repair the wrongs they have done. Even this much is called a punishment, but who can doubt that it should be deemed more a service than a severity when the rage to harm is precluded but not the prospect of a healing repentance? (L 133.1)

Augustine was very serious about this protection given to one he had most right to resent. He wrote to Marcellinus' brother, who was the proconsul of Africa, using a pragmatic argument:

> Men should read the court proceedings, to heal souls poisoned with seductive venom. Do you want, as we read to the point where a bloody severity is included in the sentence, that we should shrink from finishing? . . . As for us, if no lighter sentence were available, we should prefer to see them released rather than avenge our brother's murder by further bloodshed. (L 134.4)

Nor was this enough. When Augustine was not given a guarantee that the convicts would live, he informed Marcellinus he was instituting a plea for clemency to the emperor. No wonder some contemporaries criticized Augustine for being too lenient to Donatists (L 11.25–26).

Some have said that Augustine only wanted to prevent giving Donatists new martyrs they could rally to. That may have been one consideration, but he opposed any use of capital punishment—reversing Hamlet's calculus. Hamlet will not kill his uncle while he is praying, since he wants to catch him in sin, when death will take him straight to hell. Augustine feels that the criminal needs time to cool down, to consider, to repent, to pray. Augustine knew from his own case that God may have future uses for a sinner who renounces his sin. One must always correct out of love.

It is the corrective use of punishment that explains a dictum often criticized: *Ama et quod vis fac*—"Act as you desire, so long as you act with love." Some take that to mean that a profession of love frees one from constraint. But for Augustine love *is* the constraint. He first used the sentence when discussing the admonition of fellow Christians in his *Commentary on Paul's Letter to the Galatians* (57):

> We should never undertake the task of chiding another's sin unless, cross-examining our own conscience, we can assure ourselves, before God, that we are acting from love. If reproaches or threats or injuries, voiced by the one you are calling to account, have wounded your spirit, then, for that person to be healed by you, you must not speak till you are healed yourself, lest you act from worldly motives, to hurt, and make your tongue a sinful weapon against evil, returning wrong for

wrong, curse for curse. Whatever you speak out of a wounded spirit is the wrath of an avenger, not the love of an instructor. *Act as you desire, so long as you are acting with love.* Then there will be no meanness in what may sound mean, while you are acutely aware that you are striving with the sword of God's word to free another from the grip of sin. And if, as often happens, you begin some course of action from love, and are proceeding with it in love, but a different feeling insinuates itself because you are resisted, deflecting you from reproach of a man's sin and making you attack the man himself—it were best, while watering the dust with your tears, to remember that we have no right to crow over another's sin, since we sin in the very reproach of sin if anger at sin is better at making us sinners than mercy is at making us kind.

He also used the formula in a sermon on the First Letter of John, that broad treatment of love (JL 7.8):

Because of varying circumstances, we see one man looking harsh because he loves and another looking pleasant because of vice. The father gives a son blows, the whoremonger gives blandishments. Consider them in themselves, blows or blandishments—who wouldn't take the blandishments and duck the blows? But look at the motives—they are the blows of love, the blandishments of vice. You see my point, that human acts should be judged by their basis in love. Many things have a surface appearance of good, but are not based on love—like blossoms on a thorn plant. Other things look hard, look forbidding, but they instill a discipline informed by love. Once again, to put it simply: *Act as you desire, so long as you act with love.* If you are silent, be silent from love. If you accuse, accuse from love. If you correct, correct from love. If you spare, spare from love. Let love be rooted deep in you, and only good can grow from it.

This is hard teaching, not an excuse for repression. Even Alypius, as Brown says (233), seems not to have taken it entirely to heart. But in Marcellinus Augustine had a tribune strong yet compassionate, a seeker after the truth, to whom Augustine dedicated the first installment of *The City of God*. It is tragic that, just as Marcellinus and Augustine were fashioning the corrective discipline needed after the Confrontation of 411, the tribune was caught up in a purge after an attempted coup and was executed in 413. Augustine set in motion all the appeals for clemency that he once directed *at* Marcellinus. Now they were deployed *for* Marcellinus. Augustine visited him in prison, and hoped for an amnesty that was precluded by a hasty execution.

This was a crushing blow to Augustine, one sensitively analyzed by Brown (337):

At this crucial moment, Augustine showed that he was no Ambrose: he lacked the streak of obstinacy and confidence that he could control events that is so marked in the great ecclesiastical politicians of his age. The incident also marks, on a deeper level, the end of a period of Augustine's life. For, paradoxically, he had lost his enthusiasm for the alliance between the Roman Empire and the Catholic Church, at just the time when it had become effectively cemented. For now that he no longer needed to convince others, Augustine seems to have lost conviction himself: he fell back on more sombre views.

Augustine was already moving toward those somber views before Marcellinus' death—in the new work he dedicated to him, *The City of God*. This book germinated from the disorientation felt by Christians over the capture of Rome. Rome had, for men of that time, seemed the organizing principle of all human history. Rome gone, what sense was to be made of the world? Augustine wrote, at a first level, to dethrone the *idea* of Rome from its place in people's minds. It was never the city that could satisfy human hearts. Only the City of God can do that.

Paradoxically, he began this systematic undermining of classical culture's claims by doing his own little raid on that culture's prizes. The use of philosophy to assuage grief had become formulaic with the Greeks and Romans. It was called the *consolatio*. Augustine composes a poignant *consolatio* for those who were killed, displaced, robbed, or raped in the fall of the ancient city. He uses the form's stoic commonplaces—death is common, natural, inevitable, a thing we all must share, must undergo at some time, so no time is better or worse for it (CG 1.11). He takes the pagan dictum that what happens to the body is not important, only the mind is precious, and gives it a Christian turn: women raped in Rome's fall do not lose their chastity, which is a virtue in the soul and does not depend on how others use the body. Even if the body responded, mechanically (he refers to the self-lubrication of a woman's stimulated genitals), that does not matter if the soul withheld consent (1.16–18). No one should seek suicide for any shame imposed on them. God can forgive as well as console, but the suicide places a person beyond repentance (the same argument he uses against capital punishment). The Romans who glorified Lucretia for not living with the shame of rape were more interested in human pride than divine mercy (1.22–25). Her crime was worse than Tarquin's: "He took her body, she took her life. He raped, she murdered." (1.19)

In the second book of *The City of God,* Augustine begins what amounts to a long palinode, or "reverse song," undoing his own favorite poem, Virgil's *Aeneid.* Virgil described the gods' plan to make Rome an image of the divine order of justice. Augustine says Rome never became that, and never could have. No merely human institution can. Only the City of God has perfect order.

Then what was Rome? The polar opposite of the City of God? Augustine cannot say that, since good Christians were involved in Rome's workings—just officials like Marcellinus, powerful patrons like Melania and Pinian. Against the Donatists, Augustine had argued that the Church on earth is a mixed body, with some weeds growing amid the wheat. In the same way, worldly governments have some wheat growing among the weeds. If both are mingled, with the same two types living together, how are they to be distinguished, if at all?

Here again Tyconius comes to Augustine's aid. He, too, believed in the mixed Church. But he contrasted Christ's body (the Christian community with some sinners in it) with Satan's body (containing only sinners, though some are also mingled in with Christ's members). This is an eschatological vision of what is going on in human history—the growing toward a final harvest that separates saints from sinners.

Augustine could use this schema, but only very carefully. For one thing, it looked too much like the picture Manicheans created of two independent principles—one sheer evil, the other perfect good—at war with each other in the messy midground of human history. In his break with Manicheism, Augustine had denied that evil has any existence in itself. He held now that pure evil would erase itself—it must have a "carrier" of the good in order to exist.

So, instead of contrasting a Satanic ruler with the City of God, Augustine spoke of the City of (postlapsarian) Man, or the Earthly City—a city made possible by Adam's fall, and constituted as an actual society when Cain founded his town. Then Augustine applied to this city all the biblical symbols Tyconius had used of the Satanic realm—especially Babylon, contrasted with Jerusalem.

But this led to a problem, which readers of the early books must have pointed out to Augustine. If the City of God is contrasted with the City of Man in human history, does that mean there are *four* polities, two of men and two of angels (the unfallen angels and the devils)? At the beginning of book 12, Augustine admits that there are only two cities, the good angels in the City of God, the bad ones in the Earthly City. But that takes Augustine back to his reluctance to use Tyconius' scheme of God versus Satan.

Augustine now sees that even the hell over which Satan rules is good in its way. Even robber bands, if they function at all, have perverted good things at the basis of their power to do bad—not only their God-derived existence, but sufficient concord to act as a group, to share common risks and rewards, to perdure on the basis of cooperation. Even self-love is a love of the good things God created in the self.

Augustine is, as usual, reorienting classical thought, which based society on justice. Augustine early on calls Cicero's definition of a polity (*civitas*) mistaken. Cicero, like Plato before him, based society on its members' joint recognition of what is just (*juris consensu*, 2.21). Augustine bases society on a social agreement on "things one loves" (*rerum quas diligit*, 19.24). We see once again that Augustine gives primacy to the *will*, not the intellect, to love, not to theories of justice.

Some have taken the demotion of justice to mean a removal of justice. But Augustine always said man's actions should be just, no matter in what area, as in his famous saying "What is a political regime, when devoid of justice, but organized crime?" (CG 4.4). But remember that his definition of a society *extended to* gangs of crooks. It is broad enough to embrace relatively just and relatively unjust regimes—and to allow him to give qualified allegiance to "earthly societies." Thus he could require Christians to be good citizens, or ask officials to be impartial, however spottily their political ideals were realized.

Indeed, his definition extends even to hell, where a perverted self-love creates a perverted society. To love the self is to love that image of God one finds in the soul (Augustine's teaching in *The Trinity*). It only becomes damning when it is a self-love that turns against ("hates") God. This is a far more complex picture than that given when various sayings are taken out of their place in Augustine's dynamic picture of social reality. When he condemns the Earthly City, he is condemning the Satanic city to which the damned are tending—as when Paul uses "the flesh" to describe sensual *principle*, not the mere physical body; or as when the Bible says the world (*mundus*) is condemned, meaning by "worldliness" that which fights God's "reconciliation of the world to Himself."

Though ultimate citizenship will be in the City of God or the City of Self-Love, we cannot at the moment identify people according to that citizenship. God foreknows. We do not. Today's sinner may be tomorrow's saint, and vice versa. Visible members of the Church on earth will end up in hell. Those outside will end up in heaven. Till the final judgment, wheat and weeds grow together, often mistaken for each other. Augustine cultivates an agnosticism about the state of others' souls—which entails a reverent fear for his own safety.

Because he thinks in biblical symbols, the Augustinian analysis has a shifting, multidimensional, dynamic quality. Tyconius had shown that the same symbol—e.g., the daystar, or the mountain—can be used at times for Satan, at times for God. This frustrates those who want neat and static patterns, and who crudely hypostasize Augustine's two cities as church and state, or heaven and earth, or time and eternity. Time is shot through with eternity, invisibly, in the historic Rome or the historic Church. God and Satan have adherents jumbled through the mixtures of all society from robber bands to episcopal councils. Much of the real drama of souls takes place behind the curtains. Augustine had his own reason to say that the world is a place "where ignorant armies clash by night"—though Matthew Arnold, when he wrote those words, was announcing God's death and Augustine drew his vision precisely from his theology of a hidden God, a providence that is not manifest. According to Augustine, saints and sinners can live together precisely because they do *not* share an ultimate orientation toward justice. What they have instead, in the criss-crossing of social ties, are sufficient concrete good things to protect and love in a joint way. What was a crippling love-bond in Adam and Eve (*socialis necessitudo*) can also be the desirable concord of society.

Post-Enlightenment liberalism has achieved a different, in many ways superior, approach to tolerance. Prescinding from social bonds, which are dismissed as irrational tribalism, it tries to achieve agreement on procedural rules and impartial equity. This has wrought great things, but at a cost. When faced with the intransigence of "irrational" social ties of religion, ethnicity, patriotism, or tradition, such liberalism can do nothing but condemn in frustrated noncomprehension. The liberal plan is superior as prescription, in situations where it can work; but Augustine can be superior in *description* of all societies, those that submit to the liberal project and those that do not. There is a kind of "existential" realism to an Augustinian analysis like Cardinal Newman's, who said that concrete societies have "a certain assemblage of beliefs, convictions, rules, usages, traditions, proverbs, and principles: some political, some social, some moral; and these tending to some definite form of government and *modus vivendi,* or polity, as their natural scope" (*Who's to Blame?*). This Augustinian realism is found not only in a Catholic like Newman, but in an atheist like Hume, who describes "the social disposition of mankind, by which men are commonly much attached to their ancient government"—making it difficult, and sometimes dangerous, to end such ties ("Of the First Principles of Government"). Hume established government on societal assumptions he called "opinion," which is much like Augustine's "predilection" (*quas diligent*). The Augustinian analysis is not confined to conservatives like Hume (or Burke); it can be found in a republican like James Madison, who also embraced the practical role of socialized opinion:

> The reason of man, like man himself, is timid and cautious when left alone; and acquires firmness and confidence in proportion to the number with which it is associated. When the examples which fortify opinion are *ancient* as well as *numerous*, they are known to have a double effect. In a nation of philosophers, this consideration ought to be disregarded. A reverence for the laws would be sufficiently inculcated by the voice of enlightened reason. But a nation of philosophers is as little to be expected as the philosophical race of kings wished for by Plato. And in every other nation, the most rational government will not find it a superfluous advantage to have the prejudices of the community on its side. (*The Federalist* No. 49)

Peter Brown (R and S 43) finds an Augustinian view of the role of concrete predilections in empirical modern findings of the social sciences:

So much of our modern study in sociology and social psychology has shown the degree to which political obedience is, in fact, secured, and political society coheres, by the mediation of a whole half-hidden world of irrational, semi-conscious and conscious elements that can include factors as diverse as childhood attitudes toward authority, crystallized around abiding inner figures, half-sensed images of security, of greatness, of the good life, and, on the conscious plane, the acceptance of certain values. These make up an orientation analogous to Augustine's *dilectio*.

Augustine spent fifteen years writing the twenty-two books of *The City of God,* that "great and trying labor" (CG 1 Pref.). They were years of increasing desire for some measure of temporal peace. Augustine's hopes for enlightened leadership, first lodged in Marcellinus, then cruelly disappointed, were partly revived when another Christian official, Boniface, came to Africa in 417 as commander (count) of the Roman military force. Augustine sent him a long statement of the Donatist policy he had created for Marcellinus (L 185). Since Boniface had important frontier duties, keeping out Saharan tribes from Christian Africa, Augustine wrote for him in 418 a little treatise on military morality— war should be waged only when it is necessary to peace, and then with the minimum necessary violence; truth should be observed even toward the enemy; mercy to the vanquished precludes use of the death penalty (L 189).

Those who think Augustine took a purely negative view of earthly realms should reflect on the fact that the bishop, in his late sixties, traveled 120 miles from Hippo to meet with Boniface in order to *dissuade* the count from giving up power to become a monk. He said that preserving political order can be a godly vocation if it protects a Christian peace (L 122.3, 122.7). He would later be disappointed in Boniface, who was neither as intelligent nor as conscientious as Marcellinus, but Augustine's relation with him shows the kind of experience his theories of social organization were based on.

Power relations were also at the center of Augustine's ecclesiastical politics in this period. When Apiarius, an unruly priest excommunicated in Africa, went to Rome for reinstatement in 419, Pope Zosimus sent delegates to Africa in order to investigate. A special council was called in Carthage (220 bishops attending, which shows the gravity of the matter) to deny the pope jurisdiction. When the pope's envoys tried to defend his authority by quoting the canons of the ecumenical Council of Nicaea (325), Aurelius and Augustine showed their greater mastery of relevant documents, as they had in the Confrontation with the Donatists: Nicaea gave no authority for appeals by priests against their episcopal superiors. When the envoys challenged the Africans' documents, Augustine suggested that a special mission be sent to the East to verify the records' accuracy. The pope's delegates had to settle for that.

The Africans were courteous but firm. This was not the first time they had stymied Pope Zosimus. When, in 418, the pope exonerated Pelagius of charges of heresy, the Africans sent a secret mission to Emperor Honorius, who condemned Pelagius—a condemnation promptly echoed by a plenary council at Carthage. Zosimus was forced to back down and issue his own condemnation. Perversely, this defeat of Rome was later claimed as a victory for papal supremacy. After the pope's second, compelled decision, Augustine told his congregation:

> In this proceeding [*causa*], two council findings were sent to the Apostolic See, and a report has come back. The proceeding is ended—I wish the heresy were. (S 131.10)

That message would later be transformed by papal apologists into: "Rome has spoken, the matter [*causa*] is ended."

The treatment of Pelagius involved a power struggle at a deeper level than this fencing between Rome and Carthage. Though Augustine joined the struggle at a late stage, in 415, it had been going on for decades before his intervention, creating enmities he fell heir to. Scholars are still sorting out all the factors at play, building on Robert Evans's pioneering book *Pelagius: Inquiries and Appraisals* (1968). In Pelagius, Augustine inherited an enemy from Jerome. Though Augustine only glimpsed Pelagius in Carthage in 411, the two men had been in Rome at the same time (383–384, 387–388). That is when Jerome knew the British ascetic—well enough to ridicule his appearance later on, calling him "slantyhead" and "the fat man filled with Scottish porridge," who "waddles like a turtle."

Relations between Jerome and Pelagius worsened when Jerome heard, in Bethlehem, that Pelagius was attacking Jerome's pamphlet on Jovinian in 394. Jovinian had claimed that Christian marriage can be as meritorious as consecrated virginity. Jerome's intemperate response went so far as to call marriage evil, saying that even a later martyrdom could barely wash its taint from a woman. This effusion was too much even for Jerome's embattled Roman allies. As J. N. D. Kelly puts it (188):

> There was panic among Jerome's friends. His exaggerated claims and unbridled language, they were quick to see, were doing incalculable damage to the very cause he and they wished to uphold. Pammachus made valiant efforts to withdraw as many copies of the embarrassing pamphlet from circulation as he could.

Pelagius in Rome had absorbed many of the ideas of Rufinus' circle of educated aristocrats. Rufinus was Jerome's ex-friend, who had taken away from him a rich and holy patron, Melania, the daughter of Albina (whose husband, Pinian, narrowly escaped forceable ordination in Augustine's church after the sack of Rome).

Pelagius, like Albina, left Rome at the time of Alaric's invasion, going through Sicily toward Africa and then to Jerusalem, where Jerome renewed his attack on him in 414, calling him an "Origenist." Jerome had earlier helped begin what Brown calls the Church's first witch hunt, against Origen, the daring speculator whose Bible commentaries Rufinus had translated in Rome. When Albina, Melania, and Pinian also reached the Holy Land, Jerome won them back from Rufinus' circle—even though he had called Melania's grandmother and namesake "one whose very name reveals the depths of her black betrayal" (L 133.3; *melan* is Greek for "black").

Augustine was reluctant to get into this squabble—Brown thinks because he had heard Pelagius' virtue praised by such friends as Albina and Paulinus of Nola, who admired the Briton. Augustine may also have entertained some misgivings about having Jerome as an ally—one rarely needed enemies when Jerome was your friend. Pelagius had expressed his own sincere admiration for Augustine's earlier works, especially the dialogue *Freedom of Choice*, in a letter he sent Augustine from Jerusalem around 413. Augustine sent back a polite thank-you note, which Pelagius used two years later to show that Augustine supported him. Augustine, for whom the letter was short and perfunctory, felt Pelagius should have known he was being treated with caution.

Pelagius' less measured associate Caelestius had been condemned by the African Council in 411, for denying that Adam's sin brought death to mankind. When Marcellinus expressed concern about Caelestius' views, Augustine wrote two treatises for him in 413 to refute Caelestius' views without ascribing them to Pelagius (*What Sin Deserves* and *The Spirit and the Letter*).

But in 415 Augustine read Pelagius' own work *Nature*, which argued that Adam's fall did not cripple human nature. Pelagius' exhaustive citation of Catholic authorities seemed especially dangerous to Augustine, and he at last opened fire on Pelagius himself, answering the Briton's book *Nature* with his own *Nature and Grace*. Jerome egged Augustine on, saying they should lay aside their differences to make common cause against Pelagius (L 172.1). In 416, Jerome peppered Augustine with four letters in quick succession (only one survives; see L 19.1).

In 415, Pelagius had been declared orthodox by a Palestinian council. Jerome wanted to get a condemnation from the

West, since his own influence was not working in the East. Augustine wrote to Eastern prelates—John of Jerusalem and Cyril of Alexandria—trying to learn the council's grounds for exoneration. Convinced that the Eastern council had erred, he put into action the efficient conciliar system of Carthage, solicited Honorius' condemnation of Pelagius, and extracted the condemnation from Pope Zosimus: "The proceding is ended—I wish the heresy were." Vain wish. Augustine had entered a quagmire in which he would thrash about for the remaining fifteen years of his life.

5. Hippo: Sin, Sex, and Death (418–430)

POPE ZOSIMUS, who raised African hackles when he sent Italian envoys to deal with the troublesome priest Apiarius, was more tactful in 418 when he asked a panel of African bishops, led by Augustine, to go settle some ecclesiastical conflict in Caesarian Mauretania—a long journey west for Augustine, about eight hundred miles from Carthage (where he was attending a council), undertaken in the hot summer by this sixty-four-year-old man (Perler 346–47). The Mauretanian churches seem not to have been well organized; they had sent few bishops to the Confrontation of 411 in Carthage and none to the plenary council of 418. Augustine performed a number of tasks along his route, including promulgation of the terms of the Donatist settlement. In Caesarea itself, he held a council of Catholic and reconciled bishops. When it was discovered that the Donatist bishop Emeritus was outside in a city square, he was invited to join his brothers.

Asked to speak to the assembly, he refused. Augustine asked why he came in if he did not want to speak with them. Firm Donatists ostentatiously declined to mix with Catholic "sinners." Augustine said he meant to use no compulsion but the truth. Emeritus made the laconic reply: "The event will show whether I am conquered or conquering, whether I am conquered by truth or compelled by force." Then why did you come in? asked Augustine. "To answer your questions." "My question is: why did you come in? If you had not come in I would not have asked you this." Emeritus spoke one last enigmatic monosyllable to the stenographer: *Fac* ("Mark that"). Augustine had Alypius read the conciliatory terms for accepting back Donatist bishops with their full episcopal powers, but still got no response from Emeritus. Augustine closed the session by saying, "We must pray for him. Who knows God's intentions?" Emeritus, the most eloquent Donatist, exits history as a mute. (Monceau 6.173–89)

When at last Augustine got back to Hippo, he had been away from his church for five months, a rare occurrence for him (he never missed the Lenten and Easter periods of instruction for the candidates for baptism). He had much business to catch up on. But at just this time, more trouble was being prepared for him at the imperial court of Ravenna. There a charming and intellectual young bishop, Julian, was telling an influential nobleman, Valerius, that Augustine was still a Manichean at heart who wished to destroy the institution of Christian marriage. Valerius was a devout Christian, and married—as was Julian.

Augustine did not expect attack from this quarter. Julian was the son and son-in-law of bishops and a friend of the saintly

Paulinus of Nola. In fact, Paulinus wrote a poem for Julian's wedding to a bishop's daughter, hoping their marriage would produce a whole line of bishops. In 408, Julian's father asked Augustine for a copy of his book *Music* to give to his son, who was then a young deacon. Augustine, while sending the book, invited Julian to come visit him at Hippo—perhaps to recruit badly needed talent for the African clergy. Augustine did not know yet that Julian was contemptuous of Africa—perhaps for forcing Pope Zosimus (who had consecrated Julian a bishop by 418) to back down and condemn Pelagius. In the years of bitter verbal battle coming up, Julian took every opportunity to ridicule Augustine's "Punic donkeys"—but the aging bishop would answer him quip for quip (U 6.18):

> Don't, out of pride in your earthly ancestry, dismiss one who monitors and admonishes you, just because I am Punic. Your Apulian birth is no pledge of victory over Punic forces, where not what your ancestors have wrought but what you have thought [*non gente sed mente*] is what matters. You should fear a punitive not a Punic outcome [*poenas non Poenos*]. You cannot escape Punic thought, no matter how you boast of your own powers, for it was a Punic saint, Cyprian, who said, "We should never crow, since we are nothing."

Julian's hatred of Augustine came from the feeling that the thugs of Augustine and Jerome had hounded Pelagius out of the Church. Julian was an admirer of Pelagius and a friend of Caelestius, the Pelagian condemned in Africa. When Zosimus, too, condemned Pelagius, Julian refused to sign the ban. He left his diocese in southern Italy (Eclanum) to join other resisters in northern Italy. They issued a call for an ecumenical council to reinstate Pelagius. That is why Julian went to Valerius with tales of Augustine's hostility to marriage. Brown says of this move: "For the first, and last, time that we know of in the history of the Early Church, the clergy sought out the opinion of a married layman on the delicate issue of sex and marriage" (B and S 415). Rushing to the fray, Augustine dashed off a book to Valerius denying that he was opposed to marriage—he was going to be tarred often with the brush of Jerome's notorious statements on marriage. Julian answered with four books against Augustine's one. A collection of excerpts from this long work was prepared for Valerius (who presumably had no time to read all four books). Augustine's agents in Ravenna got a copy of the excerpts and sent them to Africa. Augustine replied instantly, since he could not tell when a copy of the complete work might be obtained. Then, when the entire book *did* arrive, he answered that as well. The war was on, and neither man would tire or give an inch till one of them died (Augustine, fifteen years into the campaign).

Though Julian's attacks exist now only in the lengthy extracts Augustine gives when trying to refute them, in one sense Julian won this war. The picture of Augustine that many people have picked up is one that Julian created, by his own words or by Augustine's repeated return to themes chosen by Julian. It is the picture of a man pessimistic about politics and other human activity, burdened with a semi-Manichean awareness of the power of evil, and haunted by a memory of sex.

Julian (and Pelagius before him) have, in the shorthand for

this controversy, been sometimes presented as defenders of sexuality. That was not their real emphasis. Both were ascetics who had forsworn sex. Pelagius, supposed defender of marriage, never married. Julian, when his marriage produced no children, became celibate (R and S 409–10). All these people shared late-antique ideals of bodily denial remote from our mentality. In fact, Pelagius considered Augustine *lax* in his view that sin is all but inescapable. In the world of disciplined aristocrats frequented by Pelagius, a sinless life was felt to be not only achievable but achieved (R and S 192–98). Augustine was "letting down the side" when he wrote that a baptized Christian cannot observe his commitments without some special grace. Baptism was itself the special grace. Pelagius, who had praised and used Augustine's earlier works, was dismayed when a friend read him a passage from the "new" book *The Testimony* in which the bishop of Hippo admits he has temptations and weaknesses that only God can counter. Pelagius shook with fury over one sentence in particular, Augustine's prayer to God, "If you will grant what you ask, you can ask what you will" (T 10.29).

The debate was not over sex in itself, but over Augustine's claim that the sexual impulse's randomness is derived from Adam's fall. Though Pelagius used the same faulty translation of Romans 5.12 that Augustine did, he did not find original sin in this verse: "Through one man sin entered the world, and through sin death, and thus it spread to all men, *and in that person* [the Greek says *'and in consequence'*] all have sinned." For Pelagius, Adam was punished for his act, but no basic change took place in his nature. Sin spread to others because he set a bad example at the outset. Sin is not "original," not "at the origin," but cumulative. The *buildup* of sin was punished by Noah's flood, and then a *correction* was sent in the Mosaic law, enabling people to see and do God's will. When a new buildup of sin occurred, the definitive liberation was effected in Christ's saving death and resurrection.

Augustine based his concept of original sin not on one Bible verse but on a reading of large problems in Scripture, on the saving role of Christ, and on the commonsense observation that there is something kinky or askew in ordinary human nature. Though Augustine is called a pessimist and G. K. Chesterton an optimist, it was Chesterton who said the reality of original sin can be observed at that point in a lovely summer afternoon when bored children start torturing the cat. A Jewish scholar tells me he thinks original sin the most self-evident concept in the whole world of thought. And Cardinal Newman said that the present mess of human society suggests it underwent "some primordial shipwreck."

That nature was created good by God, that something went wrong, that it was Adam's fault, not God's, and that Christ repairs that wrong by grace—these are the basic tenets of Augustine on original sin. Adam's sin itself had nothing to do with sex—it was an act of proud self-love in denying God's commandment. As Brown points out (B and S 399–401), what *is* original in Augustine, what sets him apart from most earlier theologians, is his claim that sex would have occurred in Eden if there had been no fall of man (others said that with no death in Eden there was no need to keep the race going by procreation). Sex was part of the good human nature created by God. It is part of the historical human nature—Jesus had semen and could have procreated if he wanted to. In *Unfinished Answer to Julian*, Augustine agrees with Julian that a Christ without virility would be without virtue (*virilitas/voluntas*, 4.49), but says that Christ's flesh was perfectly responsive to his spirit (4.47). The question was not of capacity but of choice.

Then where did the picture of Augustine's sexual pessimism come from? It arose from his characteristic emphasis on the will. Other philosophers, both Christian and pagan, had misgivings over sex because the "brainstorm" of orgasm destroyed that limpidity (*apatheia*) of the untroubled intellect which was achieved by exercises in the mind's ascent to God. Early on, that was Augustine's view, too, when the intellect held the primary place in his anthropology. In the early *Dialogues with Myself* (1.17), he says that the sex act "throws a man's mind down from its tower." But as he came to place more emphasis on the human *will*—on love as the bond of society and the definition of God—his emphasis shifted. In *The City of God*, though he makes one brief reference to the mental eclipse of orgasm (14.16), what most interests him and gets the rest of his attention is the moment of sexual arousal (or lack thereof). Nothing better showed the loss of integrity than the body's acting apart from the will's intention. He mounts an argument *a fortiori* (the "how much more" device) in three stages:

1. Man can be aroused without intending to be. This is a "symmetrical punishment" (*poena reciproca*) for Adam's sin. As he disobeyed God's will, his own body disobeys his own will.

Adam's enjoyment of Edenic sex would have been that of an integral person. The chanciness of arousal shows a loss of the integrity, the unison, of body and soul.

2. If spontaneous arousal is an appropriate punishment, *how much more* so is impotency, the body's *refusal* to be aroused when one *wants* it to be. Adam would never have been impotent when his will was to have sex.

3. If impotence in legitimate sex is an appropriate punishment, *how much more* so is the impotence of a lecher. Here not only does the body refuse to respond to the will, but "desire itself deserts desire" (*libidini libido non servit*, CG 14.17).

4. And *how much more* dramatic a sign of the disconnect between human body and human will is the *alternation* of two "malfunctionings," the body aroused when that is not wanted, and not aroused when it is:

> At times, without intention, the body stirs on its own, insistent. At other times, it leaves a straining lover in the lurch, and while desire sizzles in the imagination, it is frozen in the flesh; so that, strange to say, even when procreation is not at issue, just self-indulgence, desire cannot even rally to desire's help— the force that normally wrestles against reason's control is pitted against itself, and an aroused imagination gets no reciprocal arousal from the flesh. (CG 14.17)

This is the quandary complained of by Philip Roth's Portnoy. When he does not want an erection (as when he is told to stand in the classroom), there it is, "like some idiot macrocephalic making his private life a misery with his simpleton's insatiable needs." But when a prostitute tells him "Take it out," he can't even find it:

> "Sure, if that's what you want, here . . . here," I say, but prematurely. "I—just—have—to—get—it—" Where *is* that thing? In the classroom I sometimes set myself consciously to thinking about DEATH and HOSPITALS and HORRIBLE AUTOMOBILE ACCIDENTS in the hope that such grave thoughts will cause my "boner" to recede before the bell rings and I have to stand. It seems that I can't go up to the blackboard in school, or try to get off a bus without its jumping up and saying "Hi! Look at me!" to everyone in sight—and now it is nowhere to be found.

Augustine dwells most often on impotence, as the extreme example of inner dividedness, where desire is rebellious not only against reason but against itself. He tells of the Stoics, those professionals of shock in late antiquity, who wanted to defy codes of decency by performing sexual intercourse in public, but who—like porn actors unable to respond on cue—had to throw a cloak over themselves and use their clubs to simulate erection (CG 14.20). The detumescing effect of public nudity is also a sign that the unembarrassed possession of sexual intent in Eden has been flawed (CG 14.07). As Portnoy puts it, "Who wins an argument with a hard-on?"

The elegance of his argument about the symbolic appropriateness of impotence as a sign of man's inner dividedness after the fall made Augustine go to the very limits of decent description, as he himself admits—but he adds that even this inhibition on frank speech is a result of the fall. Adam would have had no embarrassment using even the most graphic language about sex when he was still innocent (CG 14.23).

It is the clinical precision of his language about arousal that has made some people call him "obsessed with sex." But he did not make this argument outside the context of his dispute with Julian over original sin. As Brown notes (B and S 416), he did not harp on sexual sin in preaching to his congregation. Greed, violence, and deception were greater concerns in the sermons. In his pastoral life, he was hardly a scourge of sexual sin. In fact, one can see why Pelagius called him lax. He was "surprisingly unruffled" by an accusation of sexual misconduct by a priest until overwhelming evidence was found. As Brown says: "One can imagine what Jerome would have made of the incident" (R and S 397). When a priest and a monk were accused of homosexuality, Augustine sent them to a shrine to pray for God's judgment while telling his parishioners to suspend judgment where they do not know the secrets of others' souls (L 78). On the other hand, when a monk of his monastery was found to be deceiving others about the property he held, Augustine rejected the attempt to transfer the property to the monastery, expelled the man, did an audit of others' holdings, and explained the investigation in two sermons to his people (S 355–56). Sins of calculation, cold acts like lying, were what he most castigated—Satanic sins. For sins of the flesh (which Satan, having no flesh, could not commit), his own experience did not make him intolerant but compassionate. He told his people (S 78.6), during the scandal of homosexuality in the monastery, that his motto was taken from Saint Paul: "Who is weak, and I am not weak?" (2 Corinthians 11.29).

When Chesterton's detective priest, Father Brown, is asked how he got into a criminal's mind, he says it was by knowing that he is a criminal himself. When the prophet of an exotic religion tells the priest that they share an interest in spiritual powers, he answers that he deals more with spiritual weakness. Father Brown voices good Augustinian doctrine:

> No man's really any good till he knows how bad he is, or might be; till he's realized exactly how much right he has to all this talk about "criminals," as if they were apes in a forest ten thousand miles away; till he's got rid of all the dirty self-deception of talking about low types and deficient skills; till he's squeezed out the last drop of the oil of the Pharisees; till his only hope is somehow or other to have captured one criminal, and kept him safe and sane under his own hat. (*The Secret of Father Brown*)

In his opposition to Pelagius and Julian, to their circle of wealthy scholars who claimed to be living perfect Christian lives, Augustine voiced the daily concerns of his own community of far-from-perfect Christians. He pitted their common sense against Julian's boasted mastery of Aristotelian categories, then contrasted his own flock's faith with Julian's reason: "With cocked head and smiling face you dismiss the mob, which you say is not up to the fine distinctions" of a genius like yourself (U 2.36, 51).

Brown (385) finds something demagogic in Augustine's appeal to the mob against snobs. But we have to remember that he was dealing with a man who had ridiculed "Punic [Phoenician] donkeys" and Augustine as the chief "donkey tender." It is true that there was a clash of temperaments here, as well as of tenets, a large difference in social tone. Adolf Harnack, the great historian of dogma, said of Augustine and Julian: "To appreciate the uncommon qualities of two such worthy adversaries is to wish that Nature could have combined them into one man—*what* a man *that* would be."

In this slugging match, both Julian and Augustine ended up rather punch-drunk. Each scored points that later backfired. There is a tragic hopelessness in their dreary round of repeated arguments:

> AUGUSTINE: If there is no original sin, why does your church baptize babies?
>
> JULIAN: If babies are unbaptized, do they go to hell?
>
> AUGUSTINE: If baptism does not save, why did Pelagius make it the central act of Christian life?

Or the celebrated argument on nature versus grace:

> JULIAN: If God created nature good, why does He have to rescue it all the time with last-minute graces?
>
> AUGUSTINE: Isn't God intervening all the time, even in the order of nature?
>
> JULIAN: What room does that leave for *human* responsibility and virtue?

On this last controversy, the Dominican scholar François Réfoulé has argued that Julian anticipated the great Dominican master, Thomas Aquinas, in drawing a bright line between nature and grace. That kind of division was against the whole tenor of Augustine's thought. He held that God is always creating, instant by instant; is illuminating the mind, even in "natural" thought, about spiritual things; is creating a mysterious echo of the Trinity in every intellectual creature, even Satan. Making a man live in the first place is as miraculous as making Lazarus live again. Changing water to wine by the growth and harvesting of grapes is just a "slower" miracle than that at Cana. Every spring is a resurrection. The wonders of nature always astonished Augustine. The last book of *The City of God*, written when he was seventy-one, is a long series of "ooh"s and "ah"s at creation's surprises, hints of the great surprise to come in heaven.

When he was young, the exhilaration of escaping the Manichean view of evil made Augustine celebrate existence in its lowest forms:

> I could descant in all candor on the glories of the worm, when I look at its iridescence, its perfect corporeal rotundity, its interaction of end with middle, middle with end, each contributing to a thrust toward oneness in this lowest of things, so that there is no part that does not answer to another part harmoniously. And what of the principle of life effervescing its melodious order through this body?—its rhythmic activation of the whole, its quest for that which serves its life, its triumph over or revulsion from what threatens it, its reference of all things to a normative center of self-preservation, bearing a witness

more striking than the body's to the creative unity that upholds all things in nature? (*The True Religion* 77)

Late in life, Augustine could marvel at any created thing or faculty—even farting: "Some can produce at will odorless sounds from their breech, a kind of singing from the other end" (CG 14.24). His theological point is that men can gain greater control over their farts than over their erections, but the marveling runs through all Augustine's thought on the body. In heaven, even the bowels will be beautiful, since we shall surpass the knowledge achieved by dissectors of dead bodies when we contemplate the translucent order of risen bodies (CG 22.24).

Nor was the wonder only for bodies in heaven. This man who is said to have despised the body made his great break from tradition in *rejecting* such contempt for the body. As Brown says, late-antique thought was hierarchical in its assumptions, and the body comes at the low end of the spectrum of things. It was what one had to *escape* in order to climb the long spiritual path to Wisdom. It was the darkness out of which one must wrestle one's way toward Light. It was the muddied lower end of a stream whose pure Fountain was far above it. By meditating on the fact that God became *flesh* in Jesus, Augustine turned that whole world upside-down. In a passage as packed with metaphysical "conceits" as any poem by Donne, Augustine preached the carnality of the Incarnation:

Man's maker was made man that He, Ruler of the stars, might nurse at His mother's breast; that the Bread might hunger, the Fountain thirst, the Light sleep, the Way be tired on its journey; that Truth might be accused of false witnesses, the Teacher be beaten with whips, the Foundation be suspended on wood; that Strength might grow weak; that the Healer might be wounded; that Life might die. (S 191.1)

Over and over Christ's flesh is put before his audience. It is like the paste put on blind eyes to heal them. It is like the milk by which we had life mediated to us in our infancy.

His deepening awareness of the humble mysteries of the body helps explain what many find striking, and some deplorable, in Augustine's later years: the man who had initially played down miracles, along with martyr cults, now became enthusiastic for them. A new wave of miracles came to Africa, along with relics from the Holy Land, in the 420s. Augustine accepted the view that a God who deigned to come into history in visible form was not so far "above" corporal wonders as the Neoplatonist Augustine had thought. Augustine wanted also to reconcile Donatists to the Church they had been forced (at least in theory) to join—and martyr cults were the authentic "African religion" that Donatists had been devoutly attached to. We should probably also suspect that Augustine found traces of his own earlier self in the elitist attitudes of Julian, his scorn of mob religion. The "perfect" Pelagians recall too pointedly Augustine's early call to his friends that they "divinize" themselves *(deificari)*. Augustine wanted to dissociate his later views from those that Pelagius had found in his immature dialogues. It is significant that Augustine now quotes Ambrose with increasing frequency and devotion. He tells Julian that Ambrose, too, was an aristocrat; he, like Julian, could read the Greek theologians; yet he was a pastor of mere imperfect Christians around the court in Milan, whose populace rallied to his "demagogic" hymns and martyr ceremonies.

This reassessment of his own career helped prod him into the quite laborious task of cataloging all his own writings in the monastery archive, creating a new book, *Reconsiderations*, in 426–427, when he was in his seventy-second and seventy-third years. He had nominated Eraclius to become his successor as bishop and turned over to him such onerous chores as the court of adjudication. Augustine knew he could not live much longer, and could not do in the future what he had in the past—answer requests for books, and questions about them, by people just coming across them or receiving authorized copies from Hippo itself.

Augustine's task did not resemble that of a modern author, whose works are printed in uniform formats, copyrighted, mass-produced, easily available, of generally undoubted authenticity. When someone asked Augustine for his old book *Music*, or when he sent a new acquaintance *The Testimony*, a copy had to be laboriously written out by hand. He tried to keep a stock of all his writings on hand—he had often to consult them to answer Julian and other critics. Once books were sent off—carefully, by trusted couriers; they represented a labor-intensive investment—the new owners might have them copied, sometimes in abbreviated or inaccurate forms. Texts were plastic to many pressures. They were not easily found in the local library. Augustine, remember, answered *excerpts* from Julian's four-book assault on him because he could not be sure when or how he would get somebody's manuscript copy of the entire work. And even with the best will on his part he could not make his first letter to Jerome reach its recipient—so that Jerome doubted the authenticity of the follow-up letter.

Augustine listed his works in chronological order, indicated their original length, the opening words to each, differentiating them from "pirated" or partial copies. He put each work in context, and corrected, amended, or defended aspects of the work as seen from his later vantage. This is the kind of thing he had done, letter by letter, in sending things off himself—he told Julian's father, for instance, that he no longer thought the first five books of *Music* had any value.

Despite this rounding off of his written career, Augustine was not just a retired scholar putting his papers in order. He had turned over some tasks to Eraclius, but his pastoral and administrative chores could not be entirely escaped. The political situation called for attention—the African peace was disturbed by Saharan tribes from the south. Augustine felt that his old protégé Boniface had helped bring this plague on the province. After Augustine and Alypius had persuaded Boniface to stay in secular life as a defender of the frontier, the military officer had gone back to Italy, been embroiled in court rivalries and intrigue, married an Arian wife, and returned to Africa a changed man, now publicly living with concubines and bargaining for power against his enemies in Ravenna. Augustine wrote to rebuke Boniface for his men's rapacity and plunder, misdirected toward civilians as they neglected the military foe (L 220.6). Augustine wrote this in 427, having waited until an entirely trustworthy courier could be sent, who would not let it fall into any hands but Boniface's—

Augustine would not deal a blow to morale, or weaken his personal appeal that the man repent, by making a public scandal.

Within five years of that letter, Boniface was on the run from another enemy, not Saharan tribes from the south now, but Vandals from the west, led by the Arian chief Gaiseric, whom Boniface had tried to recruit for his own struggle with the Roman court. As Numidean towns fell, Christians and their bishops flocked into Hippo, a fortified city, and Boniface himself ended up there to conduct a defense against Gaiseric's siege. The city was blockaded from the sea, and during that protracted engagement Augustine died, aged seventy-six, on August 28, 430. The siege was not raised for another year.

In the last period of his life, the aging Augustine had the comfort, which had often been a trial, of the chosen band of brothers in his monastery. His discipline aimed at amity, and he threatened to leave the table if any monk ignored the verse he had cut into its wood:

Who gnaws with envy those who are away
May not bite food or at this table stay.

But when his last illness felled him, he asked the brothers to leave him alone in his cell. This man who seems never to have been alone—whose conversion took place in the company of Alypius, whose deepest moment of mysticism took place in the company of Monnica, whose most intimate writings were dictated to ever-present scribes—was now depriving himself of all company. The brother who brought him food found him weeping. He had asked that large-lettered copies of the penitential psalms be fixed to his cell's walls for him to go over and over, lamenting sins—not, we may be sure, the long-ago sins of his youth. He tells us in book 10 of *The Testimony* that his life as a bishop was one of sin. Augustine repented the sins of his ministry, all the rancorous dividedness, all the failed efforts at love and peace, that afflicted one unable to retire into some ivory tower. We know he blamed himself for some of this—in 423, when he was turning seventy, he had offered to retire from office when a bishop he consecrated turned out to be a destructive rogue. He wrote publicly to the pope:

> I have inflicted a tragedy in my hastiness and lack of due precaution. . . . As for me, Your Beatitude, I am debating whether to resign the exercise of my bishop's office and devote myself to merited penance, tortured as I am by fear and anguish over two possible outcomes—either that I shall have to see a church of God losing its members because of a man I imprudently made a bishop, or that (may God prevent this) a whole church may be lost, along with the man himself. (L 209.1, 209.10.)

Those are the kinds of sins he went into solitude to atone for at this last opportunity.

Yet it is appropriate that he died surrounded by the laboriously traced words of Scripture. He had, all his life, been building a palace of words in which he lived, this antirhetorical rhetorician who yet saw the divine Word reflected in every word men speak or write (or even mentally formulate), a man who loved words too well, perhaps, indulging them as they frisked from him in catchy ways, curling back around and through each other, carrying heavy loads of meaning at times, or else just bubbling up in self-indulgent echoes or assonance, yet reaching us—all those words, profound or playful—with an extraordinary immediacy, even today:

> The words I am uttering penetrate your senses, so that every hearer holds them, yet withholds them from no other. Not held, the words could not inform. Withheld, no other could share them. Though my talk is, admittedly, broken up into words and syllables, yet you do not take in this portion or that, as when picking at your food. All of you hear all of it, though each takes all individually. I have no worry that, by giving all to one, the others are deprived. I hope, instead, that everyone will consume everything; so that, denying no other ear or mind, you take all to yourselves, yet leave all to all others. Nor is this done temporally, by turns—my words first going to one, who must pass it on to another. But for individual failures of memory, everyone who came to hear what I say can take it all off, each on one's separate way. (S 187.2)

BIBLIOGRAPHICAL GUIDE

INTRODUCTION

Epigraph: Karl Jaspers, *Plato and Augustine* (Harcourt, Brace & World, 1962), p. 75.

The number of Augustine's sermons: Pierre-Patrick Verbraken, *Etudes critiques sur les sermons authentiques de saint Augustin* (Instrumenta Patristica 12, 1976), p. 18.

Confession in Roman law: *Digest* of Justinian 48.18.

The psychiatrists: Charles Klingerman, "Psychoanalytic Study of the Confessions of St. Augustine" (*Journal of the American Psychoanalytic Association* 5, 1957), pp. 469 ff. R. Brändle and W. Neidhart, "Lebensgeschichte und Theologie" (*Theologische Zeitschrift* 40, 1984), pp. 157 ff.

Decorum in Roman baths: Plutarch, *The Elder Cato* 20; Cicero, *Duties* 1.35.129; St. Ambrose, *Duties* 1.18.79.

Physical *scrutatio* before baptism: Suzanne Poque, *Augustin d'Hippone: Sermons pour les pâques* (Sources chretiennes 116, 1966), p. 27.

CHAPTER I: AFRICA

Barring outsiders from fourth-century churches: Christopher Haas, *Alexandria in Late Antiquity* (Johns Hopkins University Press, 1997), p. 215; Lepelley, vol. 2, pp. 173–84.

Augustine's use of Cicero on astronomy-astrology: Maurice Testard, *Saint Augustin et Ciceron* (Etudes augustiniennes, 1958), vol. 1, pp. 101–104.

CHAPTER II: ITALY

Manicheans promote Augustine's career: S. N. C. Lieu, *Manichaeism in the Later Roman Empire and Mediaeval China* (Manchester University Press, 1985), pp. 137–38.

Augustine's marriage plans: Brent D. Shaw, "The Family in Late Antiquity" (*Past and Present* 115, 1987), pp. 33–36.

Mallius Theodore: Alan Cameron, *Claudian: Poetry and Propaganda at the Court of Honorius* (Oxford, 1970), pp. 323–38.

Tolle lege as harvest song: A. Sizoo, "Ad August. Conf. VIII, XII, 29" (*Vigiliae Christianae* 12, 1958), pp. 104–106.

Ambrose's baptismal preparations: Josef Schmitz, CSSR, *Ambrosius De Sacramentis, De Mysteriis* (Herder, 1990), pp. 7–14.

CHAPTER III: AFRICA

Importance of Tyconius to Augustine: R. A. Markus, *Saeculum: History and Society in the Theology of Augustine* (Cambridge, 1970), pp. 105–32. Text: Tyconius, *The Book of Rules*, edited by William S. Babcock (Society of Biblical Literature, Early Christian Series 7, 1989).

Jerome's lies: J. N. D. Kelly, *Jerome* (Harper & Row, 1975), pp. 64, 65, 78, 107, 149, 150, 178, 201, 239, 252; W. H. C. Frend, "Frustrated Father," *New York Review of Books*, April 29, 1976, pp. 3–4.

Wittgenstein and Russell on time in Augustine: *Philosophical Investigations*, translated by G. E. M. Anscombe (Blackwell, 1963),

p. 42; *Human Knowledge: Its Scope and Limits* (Simon & Schuster, 1948), p. 123.

Augustine on the will: Albrecht Dihle, *The Theory of the Will in Classical Antiquity* (University of California Press, 1982).

The Confrontation with the Donatists: *Gesta Conlationis Carthaginiensis, Anno 411*, edited by Serge Lancel (Corpus Christianorum, Series Latina, 1974); Brent Shaw, "African Christianity," in *Rulers, Nomads, and Christians in North Africa* (Variorum, 1995), pp. 5–34.

Council in Mauretania: *Gesta cum Emerito* (Corpus Scriptorum Ecclesiasticorum Latinorum 53).

Augustine and the papacy: J. E. Merdinger, *Rome and the African Church in the Time of Augustine* (Yale University Press, 1976), pp. 136–53.

Harnack on Augustine and Julian: Albert Bruckner, *Texte und Untersuchungen sur Geschichte der altchristlichen Literatur* 15 (Leipzig, 1897), p. 177.

Julian and Thomas Aquinas: François Réfoulé, "Julien d'Eclane," *Revue d'études anciennes* 11 (1963), pp. 42–84.

Augustine's troubles with Antonius: Robert B. Eno, S.S., *Saint Augustine, Letters*, vol. 6 (Catholic University of America Press, 1989), pp. 130–49.

CITATIONS

Works of Augustine, with actual or presumed dates (of the Common Era)

CG *The City of God* (De Civitate Dei), 413–427

G *First Meanings in Genesis* (De Genesi ad Litteram), 401–415

J *Interpreting John's Gospel* (In Joannis Evangelium Tractatus), 406–421

JL *Interpreting John's Parthian Letter* (In Epistolam Joannis ad Parthos Tractatus Decem), 406–407

L *Letters* (Epistolae), 386–430

O *Order in the Universe* (De Ordine), 386

P *Explaining the Psalms* (Enarrationes in Psalmos), 392–417

R *Reconsiderations* (Retractationes), 426–427

S *Sermons* (Sermones), 391–429

T *The Testimony* (Confessiones), 397–401(?)

Trin *The Trinity* (De Trinitate), 397–426

U *Unfinished Answer to Julian* (Contra Julianum Opus Imperfectum), 429–430

Secondary Works

A-L *Augustinus-Lexikon,* edited by Cornelius Mayer et al. (Basel: Schwabe, 1986–   )

AV   *Sancti Augustini Vita,* by Possidius, edited by Herbert T.
            Weiskotten (Princeton University Press, 1919)

B and S   *The Body and Society,* by Peter Brown (Cornell University Press, 1988)

Brown   *Augustine of Hippo,* by Peter Brown (University of California Press, 1967)

Courcelle   *Les Confessions de Saint Augustin,* by Pierre Courcelle (Etudes augustiniennes, 1962)

Evans   *Pelagius: Inquiries and Appraisals,* by Robert F. Evans (Adam and Charles Black, 1968)

Frend   *The Donatist Church,* by W. H. C. Frend (Oxford University Press, 1952)

Grilli   *Ciceronis Hortensius,* edited by Albert Grilli (Milan: Istituto editoriale cisalpina, 1962)

Lepelley   *Les Cités de l'Afrique romaine au bas-empire,* by Claude Lepelley, vols. 1–2 (Etudes augustiniennes, 1979–1981)

Mandouze   *Prosopographie chrétienne du bas-empire: Afrique, 303–533,* by André Mandouze (Centre nationale de la recherche scientifique, 1982)

Monceaux   *Histoire litteraire de l'Afrique chretienne,* by Paul Monceaux, vols. 1–7 (Paris: E. Leroux, 1901–1923)

O'Donnell   *Augustine, Confessions,* by James J. O'Donnell, vols. 1–3 (Oxford University Press, 1992)

Perler   *Les voyages de Saint Augustin,* by Othmar Perler (Etudes augustiniennes, 1969)

R and S   *Religion and Society in the Age of St. Augustine,* by Peter Brown (Harper & Row, 1972)

Recherches *Recherches sur les Confessions de Saint Augustin,* by Pierre Courcelle (Paris: Boccard, 1950)

VDM   *Augustine the Bishop,* by F. Van der Meer, translated by Brian Battershaw and G. R. Lamb (Sheed and Ward, 1961)